THE CASE OF ARCHBISHOP MARCEL LEFEBVRE

TRIAL BY CANON LAW

Charles P. Nemeth, Esquire
M.S., J.D., L.L.M.

ANGELUS PRESS
2918 TRACY AVENUE, KANSAS CITY, MISSOURI 64109

ANGELUS PRESS
2918 TRACY AVENUE
KANSAS CITY, MISSOURI 64109
PHONE (816)753-3150
FAX (816)753-3557
ORDER LINE 1-800-966-7337

ISBN 0-935952-50-0
FIRST PRINTING—February 1994

Printed in the United States of America

DEDICATION

To my oldest son
Stephen Charles
Whose soul leans to his God
Whose heart overflows with charity
Whose strength withstands evil
and welcomes the good.

CONTENTS

ACKNOWLEDGMENTS

To undertake any canonical inquiry requires a heartfelt interest. In the case of the Archbishop, my interest was high for both practical and spiritual reasons. From the date of the 1988 decree of excommunications, I was puzzled, almost beleaguered at how a censure, so seldom seen in the age of the Vatican II, could have been so vigorously executed on the likes of Marcel Lefebvre. My consternation was shared by many, both friends and foes, both modern and traditional Catholics. In this sense I acknowledge all Catholics who raised the question and urged me to complete this study.

In all of the texts I have undertaken, the help, encouragement and correction of other authors and editors were most appreciated. At the production end, my thanks go to my administrative assistant, Lisa Baker, who managed most admirably a project dependent upon multiple languages, copious authorities and a complex and often dry subject matter. While the life and time of the late Archbishop may have been vigorous, any canonical query must, at least at times, be a rather dry exposition. To all those who edited, corrected, modified or made sensible my musings, I extend my earnest gratitude.

Help with language translation, aside from the Latin, was remarkably remitted by my long-time business associate and close friend, Barthold Brizee. Mr. Brizee single-handedly tackled the French, German, Italian and combinations thereof. I have always been amazed and cordially envious of his skill in the laws of language.

This project would have been an impossibility without the resources of the Catholic University of America in Washington, D.C. Their library holdings in law are unparalleled in the Americas. My excursions to it bore productive fruits permitting this commentary the authority essential to legitimacy. On a personal front, plaudits are extended to my brother, James Nemeth, who so ably aided me during this research phase. For Jim, choosing between Marcel Lefebvre and his required examination of graduate public policy was easy. He never left the stacks that encompass, fulfill and represent the greatness of Catholicism at Catholic University of America.

Not to be forgotten, either, is the incredible and unceasing encouragement provided by the family I treasure —Jean Marie, my beloved spouse, and my wonderful children: Eleanor, Stephen, Anne Marie, Joseph, John, Mary Claire, and Michael.

Finally, my excursion into the world of canon law would not have occurred without an Archbishop whose fervor transcends the laws of the material world, whose rootedness in Catholic life and thought makes me proud to be a Catholic. His piercing and insightful critique of current state of the Church and the world we are unfortunately witnessing, causes these pages to unfold.

Charles P. Nemeth, Esquire
at Pittsburgh, PA

PREFACE

This is a canonical inquiry into the conduct of Archbishop Marcel Lefebvre who consecrated four bishops on June 30, 1988 without a papal mandate. Its purpose is to examine, assess and weigh the validity of the *latae sententiae* excommunication posed for the act of consecration under Canon 1382 of the New Code of 1983 and Canon 2370 of the 1917 Code. Accepting that the 1917 Code has been suspended, its authority will not be binding in any sense, only illustrative and precedential to some extent.

This is an exercise in strict, unbridled canonical analysis, rigidly adherent to the language of canonical precepts. Polemics are not the function of this commentary and its content will evidence no diatribes, verbal assaults and condemnations, as are at times unfortunately witnessed in the exchange between traditionalists and modernists. Whether I support or condemn the Archbishop is irrelevant to this analysis. That I love the Archbishop I'm willing to admit, though affection is not law, nor is law any form of affection.

Readers should be advised that my review is authoritative. Every reasoned voice germane to the action has been included. To those who disagree based on emotion and preconception — the canonical authority cited throughout should be your only anchor. Nothing is said in haste or ridicule — all said is at least hopefully learned.

Readers should be advised that traditional legal footnoting has been employed as governed by the Rules of the Harvard Blue Book, A Uniform System of Citation (1993). The system, after standard author introduction, lists the book, page of reference and the year of publication, e.g., T. Lincoln Bouscaren, Adam C. Ellis & Grancis N. Kroth, Canon Law: A Text and Commentary 873 (1966). In the case of periodicals, author, name of article, the volume of the periodical, the name of the periodical with the article's first page number and the page the quote is located, and date, is the order of presentation, e.g., Robert Moynihan, *The Lefebvre Schism: A Look Back,* 3 The Catholic Report 44, 45 (1993).

Charles P. Nemeth, Esquire
Pittsburgh, PA
July 30, 1993

CHAPTER 1

Introduction

I. The Church, the World, and Archbishop Marcel Lefebvre.

Any canonical or juridical examination of the actions of the late Archbishop Marcel Lefebvre on June 30, 1988 when four bishops were consecrated despite lack of papal mandate, is not possible without knowing the man. What is it that drove this man to ordain despite the lack of approval of the See of Rome? What circumstances and conditions made a man, who perceived himself as a Catholic in every sense, disregard a specific canonical requirement in the ordination of bishops? What type of man, whose words, actions and overall intent were guided by Catholicity would find papal approval an irrelevancy to his subsequent ordinations? Indeed, all canonical provisions relevant to the consecration of bishops are undeniably plain. Canon 1013 of the 1983 Code of Canon Law states:

Canon 1013 - Nulli Episcopo licet quemquam consecrare in Episcopum, nisi prius constet de pontificio mandato.[1]

No bishop is permitted to consecrate anyone a bishop unless it is first evident that there is a pontifical mandate.[2]

---

1 Code of Canon Law, Canon 1013 (1983).
2 Code of Canon Law, Canon 1013 (1983).

Failure to await the mandate is viewed as an action automatically incurring excommunication. The action triggers a *latae sententiae* penalty. Canon 1382 states unreservedly:

Canon 1382 - Espicopus qui sine pontificio mandato aliquem consecrat in Episcopum, itemque qui ab eo consecrationem recipit, in excommunicationem latae sententiae Sedi Apostolicae reservatam incurrunt.[3]

A bishop who consecrates someone a bishop and the person who receives such a consecration from a bishop without pontifical mandate incur an automatic (latae sententiae) excommunication reserved to the Apostolic See.[4]

Despite these incontrovertible provisions, Archbishop Marcel Lefebvre conducted the ordination. Was the Archbishop a contrary and difficult personality? By all accounts, his persona exemplified great spirituality and gentility. Was the Archbishop pleasured by antagonistic postures taken against the Vatican? By all accounts, his love for the Papacy, at least institutionally, was self-evident. Did the Archbishop view his role as a thorn in the side of the Vatican bureaucracy? By all accounts, it was not the Church machine that troubled him, but the philosophical and pastoral direction adopted by the Church institution as spurred on by Vatican II.

For almost three decades since the perceived or actual "renewal" of Vatican II, Archbishop Marcel Lefebvre has been a staunch critic of its "reforms". William D. Dinges personifies Marcel Lefebvre in this fashion:

He is a symbol of an era, a personification of Catholic life, an iconic embodiment of a pre-Vatican II

---

3 Code of Canon Law, Canon 1382 (1983).
4 Code of Canon Law, Canon 1382 (1983).

ethos, of certain Catholic virtues and of once-familiar ways of manifesting them.[5]

But is the Archbishop merely a sentimental relic? Catholic author Mary Gordon calls Lefebvre's actions as being partially grounded in his "romance" with the pre-Vatican II Church:

> And so *l'incident Lefebvre* engages my imagination. It inspires in me an embarrassing richness of nostalgic fantasy: sung Gregorian Masses, priests in gold, the silence of Benediction, my own sense of sanctity as an eight-year-old carrying a lily among a hundred other eight-year-olds on Holy Thursday. The Society sparks the romance of lost cause, perhaps the least dangerous romance of all. I imagine Lefebvre a gallant, clerical Charles Boyer, bathed in a clarifying bitterness.[6]

But does this form of characterization do the Archbishop justice? At first glance, neither the historical or romantic caricature is substantive enough. His critics view Lefebvrian action as the result of melancholia — a sort of sentimentalism for the nuances of pre-Vatican II life. Some have lambasted him for being in a "time warp" hanging on to outmoded liturgical approaches and being resolute without justification.[7]

To some, the Archbishop's actions rest upon a more substantive foundation. For Lefebvre, the world and the Church in it, have steadily merged. Not in the sense of a Church — state monarchy — a governance form undoubtedly preferred by his own admission, but instead, a world

---

5 William P. Dinges, *Quo Vadis Lefebvre?*, America 602 (June 18, 1988).
6 Mary Gordon, *More Catholic Than the Pope*, Harper's 58, 60 (July 1978).
7 Bob Olmstead, *The Time Warp Goes on for Chicago's Fiesty Lefebvrites*, National Catholic Register (July 17, 1988).

infused into the Church's being. In other words, the world, even as corrupted as it is, was on par with the Church. Lefebvre bristled at the collapse of the Church's pre-eminent position. He often harkened back to the French Revolution, a period signifying the beginning of the end of the Church he knew and loved:

> And it is striking to see how our fight now is exactly the same fight as was being fought then by the great Catholics of the 19th century, in the wake of the French Revolution, and by the Popes, Pius VI, Pius VII, Pius VIII, Gregory XVI, Pius IX, Leo XIII and so on, Pius X, down to Pius XII. Their fight is summed up in the Encyclical *Quanta Cura* with the *Syllabus* of Pius IX, and *Pascendi Dominici Gregis* of Pius X. These are the two great documents, sensational and shocking in their day, laying out the Church's teaching in face of the modern errors, the errors appearing in the course of the Revolution, especially in the "Declaration of the Rights of Man". This is the fight we are in in the middle of today. Exactly the same fight.[8]

In every context, the Archbishop views modernism and its tendencies as antagonistic to his conception of Catholicism and the Church. For Lefebvre, modernism is murderous to Catholicism. He stated in 1990:

> That is what killed Christendom, in all of Europe, not just the Church in France, but the Church in Germany, in Switzerland — that is what enabled the Revolution to get established. It was the Liberals, it

---

8 Marcel Lefebvre, Two Years After the Consecrations — We must Not Waiver, We May Not Compromise, Archbishop Lefebvre's address to his priests, 5 (September 6, 1990).

was those who reached out a hand to people who did not share their Catholic principles. We must make up our minds if we, too, want to collaborate in the destruction of the Church and in the ruin of the Social Kingship of Christ the King, or are we resolved to continue working for the Kingship of Our Lord Jesus Christ? All those who wish to join us, and work with us, *Deo Gratias*, we welcome them, wherever they come from; that's not a problem, but let them come with us, let them not say they are going a different way in order to keep company with the Liberals that left us and in order to work with them. Not possible.[9]

In this substantive view, Lefebvre's frame of reference is not hinged by mere sentimentality. Modernism, a view as to the liberation and enhancement of man, and in some contexts at the expense of God, had infected Church teachings and the Magisterium. Vatican II was *a priori* proof of this virus. Cistercian Bede Lackner highlights the Archbishop's incompatible view on Vatican II and the new ecclesiology that emanates therefrom:

Archbishop Lefebvre had wholly different convictions. A member of the traditionalist Coetus Internationalis Patrum, he refused to sign the *Pastoral Constitution on the Church in the Modern World (Gaudium et spes)* and the *Declaration on Religious Liberty (Dignitatis humanae)*. He also opposed ecumenism, episcopal collegiality, the reform of the liturgy, the definition of the ministry and life of priests, and other conciliar decisions. To him and his friends, the Second Vatican Council was simply an accommoda-

9 Marcel Lefebvre, Two Years After the Consecrations — We Must Not Waiver, We May Not Compromise, Archbishop Lefebvre's address to his priests, 5 (September 6, 1990).

tion to the decadent spirit of the time, brought on by the Enlightenment and its view of man and society.[10]

To democratize the Church was, by any traditional view, a means to undermine it. To change what was once unchangeable, like the Mass and the sacraments, was an attack on truth itself. While the Archbishop has long been linked to his staunch affection and dedication to the Latin Tridentine Mass, his allegiance is not strictly based on form. The Latin liturgy represented an unbroken chain of tradition, and its rituals, from his perspective, more accurately represented and signified Catholic teachings and belief. Vatican II's rejection of the Latin Mass was one of his many proofs of modernism in the Church. Jesuit Thomas Reese appreciates this tendency in Lefebvre:

> What Archbishop Lefebvre has done is to transform this estrangement — through the rhetoric of subversion, conspiracy, heresy, injustice and eschatological urgency (and with episcopal authority) — into a counter-church movement opposing those who have "infected" Catholicism from within with the "viruses" of liberalism and modernism.[11]

In a sort of battle siege bluster, Archbishop Marcel Lefebvre withstands the onslaught of attacks on tradition. Ecumenism, humanism, doctrinal ambiguity, and inventive liturgical practices all symbolize the perversion of tradition. From his establishment of a traditional order of priests, "*The Priestly Society of Saint Pius X*," to his stinging critiques, both oral and written in design, the Archbishop wished only to minimize the collapse he witnessed, that was wrought by

---

10 Bede Lackner, *Archbishop Lefebvre and His Rebellion Today*, America 5 (July 13, 1985).
11 Thomas J. Reese, *Archbishop Lefebvre: Moving Toward Schism*, America 573, 603 (June 13, 1985).

Vatican II. For Lefebvre and his followers, the Church was in a state of emergency. As a result, their intent and decision-making had a necessitous ring. To Lefebvre and his adherents, the collapse was self-evident by closing churches, a diminution of priestly functions, a precipitous decline in seminaries and their graduates, falling church attendance and membership, and dramatic doctrinal and pastoral inconsistencies in both teaching and action on part of the episcopacy. Stated succinctly, the "New" destroyed the "Old" from Lefebvre's viewpoint:

The bitter experience of more than twenty years has largely demonstrated that to argue "in an attitude of study and communication" with the Vatican was something utterly useless; the only foreseen result of the "agreement" was the reduction to silence of the unique, authorized and disturbing voice which made itself heard at the time of the general auto-demolition of the Church.[12]

An examination of Lefebvre's mental state, the intellectual framework under which he operated, is crucial to any canonical inquiry. For how the Archbishop thinks, what type of man he is, and what mental references he relies upon, illustrates his actions. Any ecclesiastical discipline is "just" only when intent can be discerned. In every sense, Archbishop Marcel Lefebvre typified himself as a defender of the faith. With immediacy, Lefebvre staves off the destruction of Catholic Life. Father François Pivert labels the times of Marcel Lefebvre *exceptional:*

---

12 Courrier de Rome, *Neither Schismatic Nor Excommunicated* in Is Tradition Excommunicated? Where is Catholicism Today?, 1, 30 (Society of Saint Pius X, ed., 1993).

| . . .la situation exceptionnelle dans laquelle nous nous trouvons a été prévue par le droit (et aussi par le Code) à ce point que l' Église, en bonne mère, nous donne elle-même, par le droit, les solutions que les évêques nous dénient.[13] | . . .the exceptional situation in which we find ourselves, has been foreseen by the right (and also the Code) to the point where the Church, being the good mother, gives us herself, by rights, the solution which the bishops deny us.[14] |

In the mind of Lefebvre, any procedural irregularity in the ordination of bishops without papal mandate, is excusable given the Church's current state. As he commented days before the consecrations:

The seminaries are empty. There is a loss of vocations. Immorality is rampant. There is a loss of Faith in general. It is a tragic situation.[15]

With this mindset, an understandable defensiveness develops in Marcel Lefebvre. Oratorian canonist T.C.G. Glover emphasizes the condition under which Lefebvre labored:

It is for the Pope and bishops to justify their actions. They have abandoned the traditional rites of Mass and the sacraments — they have allowed heresay to be taught and abuse to abound throughout the Church. Traditional Catholics have merely remained faithful to what the Church has always taught and done, and this fidelity to Tradition is the sole cause of all their problems with authority. We now have the ludicrous episode of the Holy See condemning six bishops in the Church who are clearly Catholics! There may be plenty of others, but

---

13 François Pivert, Des Sacres Par Mgr. Lefebvre. . . Un Schisme? 8 (1988).
14 François Pivert, Des Sacres Par Mgr. Lefebvre. . . Un Schisme? 8 (1988).
15 Richard N. Ostling, *The Archbishop Calls it Quits*, Time 43 (June 27, 1988).

their Catholicism is no longer manifest, and their attitude over the past twenty years puts it in doubt.[16]

While the allegation as to a "non-manifest" Catholicism seems extreme, the defensiveness of the Archbishop is not a vacuous emotion. For the man, Marcel Lefebvre, the salvaton of souls is his primary aim. As the Church weakens, his aim is undermined. As Vatican II spreads its pastoral approach, the Church's walls shake with change that is yet fully calculated. As the episcopacy vacillates and demurs to any line of doctrinal reasoning, the saving of souls becomes less of a possibility. In the world of Marcel Lefebvre, the Church's foundation is crumbling:

Well, we find ourselves in the same situation. We must not be under any illusions. Consequently, we are in the thick of a great fight, a great fight. We are fighting a fight guaranteed by a whole line of Popes. Hence, we should have no hesitation or fear, hesitation such as, "Why should we be going on our own? After all, why not join Rome, why not join the Pope?" Yes, if Rome and the Pope were in line with Tradition, if they were carrying on the work of all the Popes of the 19th and the first half of the 20th century, of course. But they, themselves, admit that they have set out on a new path. They, themselves, admit that a new era began with Vatican II. They admit that it is a new stage in the Church's life, wholly new, based on new principles. We need not argue the point. They say it themselves. It is clear. I think that we must drive this point home with our people, in such a way that they realize their oneness with the

16 T.C.G. Glover, *Schism and Archbishop Lefebvre* in Is Tradition Excommunicated? Where is Catholicism Today?, 97, 101 (Society of Saint Pius X, ed., 1993).

Church's whole history, going back well beyond the Revolution. Of course. It is the fight of the City of Satan against the City of God. Clearly. So we do not have to worry. We must after all trust in the grace of God.[17]

---

17 Marcel Lefebvre, Two Years After the Consecrations — We Must Not Waiver, We May Not Compromise, Archbishop Lefebvre's address to his priests, 2 (September 6, 1990).

CHAPTER 2

The Consecrations

I. The Archbishop, Rome, and the Act of Consecration

A. Rome, Lefebvre, and Pope Paul VI

At the heart of the canonical inquiry is the action alleged to have been a canonical violation, namely, the ordination of four bishops without pontifical mandate. Background events and historical circumstances can illuminate the context of the Archbishop's conduct.

The Archbishop's relationship with Rome had been somewhat adversarial since his attack on the Church of the Second Vatican Council in 1974. His relationship with Pope Paul VI was unusually strained. The Pontiff labeled Lefebvre's adherence to tradition a "warped ecclesiology". In correspondence of October 11, 1976 to the Archbishop, the Pontiff relayed:

> Finally, your behavior is contradictory. You want, so you say, to remedy the abuses that disfigure the Church; you regret that authority in the Church is not sufficiently respected; you wish to safeguard authentic faith, esteem for the ministerial priesthood and fervor for the Eucharist in its sacrificial and sacramental fullness. Such zeal would, in itself, merit

our encouragement, since it is a question of exigencies which, together with evangelization and the
unity of Christians, remain at the heart of our preoc-
cupations and of our mission. But how can you, at
the same time, in order to fulfill this role, claim that
you are obliged to act contrary to the recent Council,
in opposition to your brethren in the episcopate, to
distrust the Holy See itself — which you call the
"Rome of the neo-modernist and neo-Protestant tendency" — and to set yourself up in open disobedience to us? If you truly want to work "under our
authority", as you affirm in your last private letter, it
is immediately necessary to put an end to these am-
biguities and contradictions.[18]

Lefebvre's stinging opinion of Vatican II was justified in
his view by its pastoral, rather than dogmatic design. This
being so, the Archbishop felt less restrained in his advocacy
of its errancy. To this, Pope Paul VI reacted with vigor:

Again, you cannot appeal to the distinction between what is dogmatic and what is pastoral, to
accept certain texts of the Council and to refuse others. Indeed, not everything in the Council requires
an assent of the same nature: only what is affirmed
by definitive acts as an object of faith or as a truth
related to faith requires an assent of faith. But the rest
also forms part of the solemn magisterium of the
Church, to which each member of the faithful owes a
confident acceptance and a sincere application. You
say, moreover, that you do not always see how to
reconcile certain texts of the council, or certain dispo-
sitions which we have enacted in order to put the

18 Note, *Archbishop Lefebvre, The Time for Decision*, 75 Canon Law Society, Great
    Britain & Ireland Newsletter 14, 25 (1988).

Council into practice, with the wholesome tradition of the Church and, in particular, with the Council of Trent or the affirmations of our predecessors. These are for example: the responsibility of the College of Bishops united with the Sovereign Pontiff, the new *Ordo Missae*, ecumenism, religious freedom, the attitude of dialogue, evangelization in the modern world. . . It is not the place, in this letter, to deal with each of these problems.[19]

As the troublesome dialogue continued, Lefebvre continued his seminary in Ecône, Switzerland. As their disagreements festered, Pope Paul VI forebade Lefebvre the right to ordain priests.

The Archbishop, nevertheless, ordained 13 priests. At the beginning of July, the Vatican Congregation for Bishops contacted the Archbishop and gave him ten days to abandon his intransigent position. During this period, he wrote to the Pope a letter which expressed once again his attitude of resistance. As a result, the Congregation for Bishops informed him of his suspension *a divinis* on 24 July 1976.[20]

B. Lefebvre and the New Pope: John Paul II

After his suspension, communication with the Vatican basically ceased until the death of Paul VI. In 1979, at the request of the new pontiff, John Paul II, meetings took place with the Archbishop and efforts to again regularize were undertaken. Pope John Paul II was generally considered far more sympathetic to the cause of the Archbishop than his predecessor. By 1984, the Tridentine Mass was reauthorized by the Pope, though it is arguable that the Mass was ever

---

19 Note, *Archbishop Lefebvre, The Time for Decision*, 75 Canon Law Society, Great Britain & Ireland Newsletter 14, 28 (1988).
20 Note, *Archbishop Lefebvre, The Time for Decision*, 75 Canon Law Society, Great Britain & Ireland Newsletter 14, 19 (1988).

deauthorized.

A dialogue between the Congregation of Faith developed after 1985 involving the Archbishop's rejection of certain Vatican II teachings. By 1987, at an advanced age, the Archbishop, desirous of continuing the work of his *Priestly Society of Saint Pius X*, announced his intention to ordain bishops. For the Vatican, the matter of ordination was inexorably tied to canonical obedience and a sincere recognition of Vatican II. Cardinal Gagnon conducted an Apostolic visitation to the seminary at Ecône, Switzerland on October of 1987, announcing his and the Supreme Pontiff's desire to making all things regular. The Cardinal qualified his desire by:

> [T]he hoped for definitive solution is based on the presupposition that there exists the obedience due to the Supreme Pontiff and loyalty to the magisterium of the Church.[21]

After Gagnon's apostolic visitation, "the Holy Father, in his letter of 8 April to Cardinal Ratzinger, Prefect of the Congregation for the Doctrine of the Faith, made quite clear his wish that everything possible might be done to respond to the overtures apparently being made by Archbishop Lefebvre so that the Society might be allowed to assume an authorized position within the Church in full communion with the Holy See. To advance this process, meetings were held between 12-15 April in which theologians and canonists of the Congregation and the Society took part. Satisfactory progress in these discussions made it possible for a further meeting to be held on 4 May at which the Archbishop and Cardinal Ratzinger took part. That meeting produced a protocol that was signed by both parties on 5 May. (The entire text of the protocol is included at *Appendix A*.) The

---

21 Note, *Archbishop Lefebvre, The Time for Decision*, 75 Canon Law Society, Great Britain & Ireland Newsletter 14, 20 (1988).

documents, mutually agreed, as a basis for reconciliation, had to be submitted to the Holy Father for his final approval."[22]

C. The Protocol of May 5, 1988

Discussions and background negotiations regarding the May 5th, 1988 protocol have conflicting versions. There are no qualms about the content of the protocol which included these criteria:

a) to promise loyalty to the Catholic Church and to the Roman Pontiff as head of the College of Bishops;

b) to accept the teaching contained in No.25. of the Dogmatic Constitution of the Church, *Lumen Gentium*, concerning the magisterium of the Church and the necessary adherence to it;

c) to commit themselves to study and to consultation with the Holy See — avoiding all polemics — on those doctrinal positions which to them seem difficult to reconcile with tradition;

d) to recognize the validity of the Mass and sacraments celebrated in accordance with the rites approved by Paul VI and John Paul II;

e) to promise acceptance of the normal discipline of the Church and of Church laws, especially those contained in the Code of 1983 with due regard for the special provisions made for the Society on certain matters.[23]

In exchange for this obedience, the Vatican agreed to the following:

---

22 Note, *Archbishop Lefebvre, The Time for Decision*, 75 Canon Law Society, Great Britain & Ireland Newsletter 14, 31 (1988).
23 Note, *Archbishop Lefebvre, The Time for Decision*, 75 Canon Law Society, Great Britain & Ireland Newsletter 14, 32 (1988).

a) the Priestly Society of Saint Pius X would set up as a society of apostolic life of pontifical right with approved statutes in line with Canons 731-746 and would be granted certain exemptions in respect of public worship, the care of souls and apostolic activity, regard being had to canons 679-683;

b) the Society would be given the faculty to retain the liturgical books in use until the post-conciliar reforms;

c) to coordinate relations between the various departments of the Roman Curia and diocesan bishops and to settle possible future problems and disputes, the Holy Father would set up a Roman Commission which would include two members of the Society and have the necessary faculties;

d) finally, given the unusual situation of the Society, it is proposed to the Holy Father that he nominate a bishop chosen from among its members who should not normally be the superior general.[24]

Undeniably, Lefebvre's concessions were hard fought and most likely begrudgingly given. As for the Vatican, its concessions were an easier pill to swallow especially in light of their ambiguity and indeterminacy. While item (d) above, as to Lefebvre's right to ordain a bishop, was a desirable compromise, for Lefebvre it was only a partial remedy. One bishop was insufficient for the growing work of the Society. As to the entire protocol, it appears, by all sources, that Marcel Lefebvre placed his signature. By the account of Joseph Cardinal Ratzinger, Lefebvre took only fifteen minutes to review the protocol and inscribe his signature.[25]

---

24 Note, *Archbishop Lefebvre, The Time for Decision*, 75 Canon Law Society, Great Britain & Ireland Newsletter 14, 32-33 (1988).
25 Robert Moynihan, *The Lefebvre Schism: A Look Back*, 3 The Catholic Report 44, 45 (1993).

So convinced were Vatican officials that a reconciliation had been accomplished that the following press release, authored, but never sent, was prepared:

> Following the Apostolic Visitation of His Eminence Cardinal Edouard Gagnon to the Priestly Society of Saint Pius X and in conformity with the desire expressed by the Holy Father in his letter to Cardinal Ratzinger dated April 8, 1988, there have been meetings held recently in Rome between the interested parties. The discussions were concluded with the participation of His Eminence Cardinal Joseph Ratzinger, Prefect of the Congregation for the Doctrine of the Faith, and of His Excellency Archbishop Marcel Lefebvre, Founder of the Society. An agreement on essential points was reached, and this makes it possible for a formal act of reconciliation with the related canonical consequences to be foreseen for the near future.[26]

D. The Archbishop's Misgivings

If the Vatican was assured, Archbishop Lefebvre apparently had misgivings. These doubts were based largely on his personal inability to compromise conviction and the sloth-like pace the Vatican adopted in his attempts to ordain bishops.

Vatican reticence to accommodate the set June 30, 1988 ordination deadline, triggered mistrust in an already suspicious Lefebvre. On the one hand, Lefebvre had sent numerous dossiers on Society priests recommended to the episcopacy only to have Vatican inaction lead to an assumption of denial. Indeed there are some who assert that the

---

26 Robert Moynihan, *The Lefebvre Schism: A Look Back,* 3 The Catholic Report 44, 45 (1993).

Vatican could not find one suitable candidate amongst Society priests.[27]

A day after the signing of the protocol, Lefebvre corresponded with Ratzinger and hinted at his dissatisfaction:

Your Eminence,

Yesterday, it was with true satisfaction that I placed my signature on the protocol elaborated in the preceding days. But, you yourself said you felt a deep sense of disillusionment reading the letter which you forwarded to me advising me of the response of the Holy Father on the subject of the Episcopal consecration.

In fact, postponing the Episcopal consecration to a later date not yet fixed would mean this is the fourth time that I would be postponing the consecration. It was made quite clear in my earlier letters that the date of June 30 was the latest one acceptable.

I sent you a first dossier concerning the candidates; there are still almost two months to establish the mandate.

Given the special circumstances of this case, the Holy Father could quite easily shorten the procedure in order that the mandate be communicated to us by mid-June.

If the response were negative, I would be obliged, in conscience, to proceed to the consecration, relying on the agreement given by the Holy See in the protocol to the consecration of a bishop who was a member of the Society.

The hesitations expressed on the subject of the Episcopal consecration of a member of the Society,

27 Robert Moynihan, *The Lefebvre Schism: A Look Back*, 3 The Catholic Report 44, 45 (1993).

both in writing and in conversation, cause me to have a legitimate fear of further delays. Everything has already been prepared for the ceremony on June 30; hotels, means of transport, the immense tents which will be set up for the ceremony, have all been rented.

The disillusionment of our priests and our faithful would be very great. All hope that this consecration will come about with the agreement of the Holy See, but, already disillusioned by previous delays, they would not understand if I accept a further delay. They are conscious and concerned above all about the need to have true Catholic bishops to transmit to them the true Faith to communicate to them, in a way that is certain, the graces of salvation which they aspire to for themselves and for their children.

In the hope that this request will not be an insurmountable obstacle to the reconciliation taking place, I pray, Eminence, that you accept my respectful and brotherly sentiment in Christ and Mary.

Marcel Lefebvre
Archbishop Emeritus of Tulle[28]

If words can mirror Lefebvre's intent, the letter illuminates much. The Archbishop poses the argument of *legitimate fear about further delays*. In others words, he initially sets out a rationale for the consecration of bishops based in the Vatican's irregularity and recalcitrance in approval. Second, the Archbishop advocates ordinations, despite lack of papal mandate because of the pressing need for souls' salvation. The procedural machinations of papal mandate cannot be deleterious to souls.

28 Letter from Marcel Lefebvre, Archbishop Emeritus of Tulle, to Cardinal Joseph Ratzinger (May 6, 1988) as recorded in 3 The Catholic Report 47 (June 1993).

E. The Vatican's Reaffirmation of the Protocol

In response, Cardinal Ratzinger replied instantaneously, urging the Archbishop to conform his decision-making to the protocol:

> Given that these intentions are in very sharp contrast with what you accepted during our conversation on May 4 and agreed to in the protocol which you signed yesterday, I would like to inform you without delay that the publication of the planned press communiqué must, for the moment, be postponed.
>
> I deeply hope that you will reconsider your position in conformity with the results of our discussions, in such a way that the communiqué can be released.

F. The Archbishop's Decision

On June 2, 1988, the Archbishop corresponded directly with the Pope concerning this and other matters. In a tone defiant of not the papacy, but the current infection of modernism, Lefebvre challenges the papacy's refusal to act on requests for Society candidates for the episcopacy.

Etant donné le refus de considérer nos requêtes et étant évident que le but de cette réconciliation n'est pas du tout le même pour le Saint-Siège que pour nous, nous croyons préférable d'attendre des temps plus propices au retour de Rome à la Tradition.[29]

Since our requests have been refused and since it is obvious that the Holy See and ourselves view in a different light the purpose of any reconciliation, we believe it is better for us to wait for the time when Rome might readily return to the true tradition.[30]

29 Note, *Lo Scisma Di Lefebvre*, LXI Apollinaris 529, 537 (1988).
30 Note, *Archbishop Lefebvre, The Time for Decision*, 75 Canon Law Society, Great Britain & Ireland Newsletter 14, 34-35 (1988).

Then, aware of the necessary pontifical mandate, Lefebvre ingenuously deduces that prior arguments, both orally and in writing, indicate a papal willingness to permit the consecrations:

C'est pourquoi nous nous donnerons nous-mêmes les moyens de poursuivre l'Oeuvre que la Providence nous a confiée, assurés par la lettre de Son Eminence le Cardinal Ratzinger datée du 30 mai, que la consécration épiscopale n'est pas contraire à la volonté du Saint-Siège, puisqu'elle est accordée pour le 15 août.[31]	That is why we will provide ourselves with the means to foster the work that providence has entrusted to us, acting on the assurances given by Cardinal Ratzinger in his letter on 30 May that the episcopal consecration is not contrary to the mind of the Holy See since it would have been willing to grant it on 15 August.[32]

Other relevant portions of the letter are reproduced below:

The discussions and negotiations we have held with Cardinal Ratzinger and his colleagues, though conducted throughout with courtesy and kindliness, have convinced us that the time for sincere and effective collaboration has still not arrived.

Indeed, if every Christian is entitled to ask of the Church authorities due protection for his or her baptismal faith, what can priests and religious men and women say?

It is with the intention of keeping intact the Faith into which we were baptized that we have felt ourselves obliged to resist the spirit and reforms of the Second Vatican Council.

False ecumenism is at the root of all the Council's innovations: in the liturgy, in changed relationships between the Church and the world, in the very self-

31 Note, *Lo Scisma Di Lefebvre*, LXI Apollinaris 529, 537 (1988).
32 Note, *Archbishop Lefebvre, The Time for Decision*, 75 Canon Law Society, Great Britain & Ireland Newsletter 14, 34-35 (1988).

understanding of the Church itself; it is leading the
Church into ruin and Catholics to apostasy.

Radically opposed to this destruction of our Faith
and determined to stay faithful to the doctrine and
traditional discipline of the Church especially in all
that concerns priestly formation and religious life, we
feel the absolute need to have from ecclesiastical
authority a sympathetic appreciation of our anxieties
and support for our efforts to counter the spirit of
Vatican II and that of Assisi.

That is why we have asked for several bishops
chosen from among those who accept the tradition
and for a majority in the Roman Commission. It is to
defend ourselves against the danger of compromise.

We shall continue to pray that today's Rome,
infected with Modernism, may become again Catholic Rome and rediscover its tradition of two millen-
nia. Then there will be no need for any reconciliation
and the Church will rediscover its youthful vitality.

Please accept, Holy Father, my best respects and
my filial devotion in Jesus and Mary.[33]

G. Papal Correspondence with the Archbishop

On June 9, 1988, the Sovereign Pontiff, John Paul II responded to the Archbishop. The frustration of the Pope is
evident in his characterization of "deep and acute distress"
(profonde affliction que j'ai pris connaisance). The Pontiff sets
out those steps relevant to the signing of the protocol of May
5, 1988. In an emotional attempt to rein in the Archbishop,
the Pope remarked:

---

33 Note, *Archbishop Lefebvre, The Time for Decision,* 75 Canon Law Society, Great
Britain & Ireland Newsletter 14, 34-35 (1988).

D'un coeur paternel, mais avec toute la gravité que requièrent les circonstances présentes, je vous exhorte, Vénérable Frère à renoncer à votre projet qui, s'il est réalisé, ne pourra apparaître que comme un acte schismatique dont les conséquences théologiques et canoniques inévitables vous sont connues. Je vous invite ardemment au retour, dans l'humilité, à la pleine obéissance au Vicaire du Christ.[34]	With a paternal heart, but with all the gravity which the present circumstances require, I exhort you, Venerable Brother, to renounce your project, which, if it is realized, could only appear as a schismatic act, the theological and inevitable canonical consequences of which are known to you. I ask you ardently to return, in humility, to full obedience to the Vicar of Christ.

At the same time, the Pope, as required by canon law precepts, officially warned *(monitum)* the Archbishop of the serious canonical consequences if he proceeded with the ordinations. The Pope labeled the actions "schismatic." The entire text of the Pope's last and unsuccessful correspondence is below:

I received your letter of 2 June with deep and acute distress.

In striving to maintain the unity of the Church in fidelity to the revealed truth — a demanding burden placed in the successor of Peter — I arranged last year for an apostolic visitation of the Fraternity of Saint Pius X and its works to be carried out by Cardinal Edouard Gagnon. Consultations followed first with experts for the Congregation for the Doctrine of the Faith and then between Cardinal Ratzinger and yourself. In the course of these negotiations, some solutions were worked out, agreed and signed by you on 5 May 1988. These allowed the Society of Saint Pius X to exist and work within the Church in full communion with the Sovereign Pontiff, guardian of unity in the truth. For its part, the Holy See had but one

---

34 Note, *Lo Scisma Di Lefebvre*, LXI Apollinaris 529, 537 (1988).

objective, to foster and safeguard that unity in obedience to divine revelation, translated and interpreted
by the Church's magisterium especially in the
twenty-one ecumenical councils from Nicea to the
Second Vatican Council.

In the letter you addressed to me, you seem to
have gone back on all previous conversations since
you clearly intend to give yourself "the means to
foster your work", notably by means of one or more
episcopal ordinations without apostolic mandate.
All this flagrantly contradicts the prescriptions of
Canon Law but also the protocol signed on 5 May and
the guidelines for this problem that Cardinal Ratzinger laid out in the letter he wrote to you at my request
on 30 May.

From the depths of my fatherly heart but with all
the seriousness that present circumstances demand,
I beg you, Venerable Brother, to renounce your present intention which if realized has to appear as a
schismatic act whose inevitable theological and canonical consequences are well known to you. I beg
you urgently to return in humility to full obedience
to the Vicar of Christ.

Not only do I invite you to this but I beg you by
the wounds of Christ our Redeemer, in the name of
Christ who on the night before he suffered prayed for
his disciples "that they might be one" (Jn. 17:20).

To this plea and this invitation I join my daily
prayer to Mary, Mother of Christ.

Dear Brother, do not allow this year dedicated in
a special manner to the Mother of God to inflict a new
wound in her maternal heart.[35]

---

35 Note, *Archbishop Lefebvre, The Time for Decision*, 75 Canon Law Society, Great
Britain & Ireland Newsletter 14, 36-37 (1988).

An official monitum, dated June 17, 1988, was
sent by Cardinal Bernard Gantin of the Congregation
of Bishops. The monitum cites relevant canonical
provisions, namely Canons 1013 and 1382. The
warning that is in Italian with the English translation,
is below:

Ecc.mo e Rev.mo Mons. Marcel Lefebvre, Arcivescovo-Vescovo Emerito di Tulle,

Poiché il giorno 15 del corrente mese di giugno hai dichiarato di voler ordinare Vescovi quattro presbiteri senza aver prima richiesto il mandato del Sommo Pontifice di cui al canone 1013 del Codice di Diritto Canonico, ti invio questa pubblica canonica ammonizione, confermando che se porterai a compimento un tale progetto, tu stesso e i Vescovi da te ordinati incorrerete *ipso facto* nella scomunica *latae sententiae*, riservata alla Sede Apostolica, secondo il canone 1382.

Perciò ti scongiuro e ti supplico nel nome di Gesù Cristo, di riflettere seriamente se ciò che stai per intraprendere contro le leggi della sacra disciplina, e su tutti i gravissimi effetti che ne derivano contro la stessa communione delle Chiesa Cattolica di cui tu stesso sei Vescovo.

Dato a Roma dalla sede della Congregazione per i Vescovi, il 17 Giugno 1988.

Per mandato del Sommo Pontefice.

Card. Bernardin Gantin
Prefetto della Congregazione[36]

To His Excellency the Most Reverend Mons. Marcel Lefebvre, Archbishop-Bishop Emeritus of Tulle,

Since on the 15th day of the current month of June you have declared that you wish to ordain as bishops four priests without having first received the mandate of the Supreme Pontiff, in accordance with canon 1013 of the *Code of Canon Law*, I send you this public canonical admonition, confirming that if you carry out the aforesaid project you yourself and the four bishops ordained by you will incur *ipso facto* the excommunication *latae sententiae* reserved to the Apostolic See according to canon 1382.

For this reason I beg and supplicate you in the name of Jesus Christ, that you reflect profoundly upon the act you are about to perform against the laws of holy discipline and upon the very grave effects that will follow from that in regard to the very communion of the Catholic Church, of which you yourself are a bishop.

Given at Rome, by the Congregation for Bishops, on June 17, 1988.

By mandate of the Supreme Pontiff

Bernardin Cardinal Gantin
Prefect of the Congregation[37]

---

36 Note, *Lo Scisma Di Lefebvre*, LXI Apollinaris 529, 537 (1988).
37 Robert Moynihan, *The Curia's Dilemma*, Inside the Vatican 8, 16 (Aug./Sept. 1993).

But the Archbishop's course had dramatically been altered. On June 19, 1988, a communique was issued to his followers that affords an understanding of his views of the protocol:

> The talks that followed in April and May disappointed us very much. A doctrinal text was presented to us, the 1983 *Code of Canon Law* was added to it, Rome reserved for itself five members of the seven on the Roman Commission, including the President (who will be Cardinal Ratzinger) and the Vice-President.
>
> The question of the bishop was only resolved with great difficulty: they insisted on trying to show us that we did not need a bishop.
>
> The cardinal then informed us that we would have to allow one new Mass to be celebrated at St. Nicolas du Chardonnet. He insisted on the one and only Church, that of Vatican II.
>
> Despite these disappointments, I signed the protocol on May 5. But already the date of the episcopal consecration constituted a problem. Then came the draft of a letter asking pardon of the Pope, which was put into my hands.
>
> I found myself constrained to write a letter threatening to carry out the episcopal consecrations in order to receive the date of August 15 for the episcopal consecration.
>
> The climate is absolutely not one of fraternal collaboration and of a pure and simple recognition of the Society. For Rome, the aim of the talks is reconciliation, as Cardinal Gagnon says, in an interview he granted to the Italian newspaper *Avenire*, that is, the return of the lost sheep to the fold.

This is why I say in the letter I sent to the Pope on June 2: "The aim of the talks is not the same for you and for us."[38]

One final futile effort by Cardinal Ratzinger consisted of a telegram sent on June 29. The Cardinal beseeches Lefebvre to cease the ordination and to remain faithful to the Pope. The telegram is published below.

Per amore di Cristo e della sua Chiesa, il Santo Padre le chiede paternamente e fermamente di partire oggi stesso per Roma senza procedere il 30 giugno alle ordinazioni episcopali de lei annunciate. Egli prega i santi apostoli Pietro e Paolo affinché la ispirino a non tradire l'episcopato di cui lei ha ricevuto l'ufficio, né il giuramento da lei pronunciato di rimanere fedele al Papa, successore di Pietro. Egli domanda a Dio di guardarla dal non conservare e disperdere quello che Gesù Cristo è venuto a radunare nell'unità. Egli la affida all'intercessione della SS. Vergine Maria, Madre della Chiesa.

Joseph Card. Ratzinger
28 Giugno 1988[39]

For the love of Christ and of his Church, the Holy Father asks you paternally and firmly to leave this very day for Rome without proceeding on June 30 to the episcopal ordinations you have announced. He prays the holy Apostles Peter and Paul to inspire you not to betray the episcopate of which you have received the ministry or the oath that you pronounced to remain faithful to the Pope, Successor of Peter. He asks God to prevent you from leading astray and scattering those when Jesus Christ came to gather into unity. He entrusts you to the intercession of the Most Holy Virgin Mary, Mother of the Church.

Joseph Cardinal Ratzinger
28 June 1988[40]

H. The Ordination and Papal Reaction

Despite these pleas and admonitions, Archbishop Marcel Lefebvre proceeded with the planned ordinations on June 30, 1988.

The Vatican response to the ordinations was swift and unequivocal. A decree by Cardinal Gantin of the Congregation of Bishops made formal the *latae sententiae* excommuni-

---

38 Robert Moynihan, *The Curia's Dilemma,* Inside the Vatican 8, 15 (Aug./Sept. 1993).
39 Joseph Ratzinger, *Telegramma* in Apollinaris 545 (1988).
40 Joseph Ratzinger, *Telegram* in Inside the Vatican 22 (Aug./Sept. 1993).

cation and curiously declared that anyone who follows the Society priests is *ipso facto* a schismatic.

Sacerdotes et Christifideles monentur ne schismaticae Domini Lefebvre actioni assentiantur, ne in eandem poenam incurrant" [41]	The priests and faithful are warned not to seek to adhere to the schism of Monsignor Lefebvre, because they would incur *ipso facto* the extremely grave penalty of excommunication.[42]

On July 2, 1988, by motu proprio, *Ecclesia Dei Afflicta,* the Pope pronounced the canonical consequences of the Archbishop's conduct and remedial steps to draw back in those it now characterized as "schismatic." As to the canonical findings and penalties, the motu proprio holds:

Quam ob rem talis inoboedientia — secum quae infert veram repudiationem Primatus Romani — actum *schismaticum* efficit. Atque eundem peragentes actum, quamquam publicum *monitum* ad illos deferendum curaverat Cardinalis Praefectus Congregationis pro Episcopis superiore die decimo septimo mensis Iunii, Reverendissimus Dominus Lefebvre necnon sacerdotes Bernardus Fellay, Bernardus Tissier de Mallerais, Richardus Williamson et Alfonsus de Galarreta in gravem incurrerunt excommunicationis poenam iam ecclesiastica disciplina praestitutam. [43]	In itself, this act was one of disobedience to the Roman Pontiff in a very grave matter and of supreme importance for the unity of the Church, such as is the ordination of bishops whereby the apostolic succession is sacramentally perpetuated. Hence such disobedience — which implies in practice the rejection of the Roman primacy — constitutes a schismatic act. In performing such an act, notwithstanding the formal canonical warning sent to them by the Cardinal Prefect of the Congregation for Bishops on 17 June last, Msgr. Lefebvre and the priests Bernard Fellay, Bernard Tissier de Mallerais, Richard Williamson and Alfonse de Galarreta, have incurred the grave penalty of excommunication envisaged by ecclesiastical law.[44]

41 Note, *Lo Scisma Di Lefebvre,* LXI Apollinaris 529, 551 (1988).
42 Bernardin Gantin, *Decree of Declaration of Excommunication of the Congrepation of Bishops,* Inside the Vatican 12 (Aug./Sept. 1993).
43 Acta Apostolicae Sedis - Commentarium Officiale, 1496 (Nov. 15 1988).
44 Johannes Paulus II, *The Apostolic Letter Ecclesia Dei,* Inside the Vatican 20 (Aug., Sept. 1993).

The Pope makes plain that the ordination is an act of *grave* disobedience, and by implication a schismatic act. By the act of ordination, both the Archbishop and the priests so ordained to be bishops, "incurred the grave penalty of excommunication envisaged by ecclesiastical law." The *motu proprio* then describes the "incomplete and contradictory" perception of tradition held by Lefebvre.

Huius autem schismatici actus *radix* dignosci potest in ipsa aliqua imperfecta et pugnanti sibi notione Traditionis:

Imperfecta, quandoquidem non satis respicit indolem *vivam* eiusdem Traditionis, quae -- uti clarissime docet Concilium Vaticanum Secundum -- (est ab Apostolis ... sub assistentia Spiritus Sancti in Ecclesia proficit: crescit enim tam rerum quam verborum traditorum perceptio, tum ex contemplatione et studio credentium, qui ea conferunt in corde suo, tum ex intima spiritualium rerum quam experiuntur intellegentia, tum ex praeconio eorum qui cum episcopatus successione charisma veritatis certum acceperunt).

Sed omnino discors est pugnans Traditionis notio quae universali Ecclesiae Magisterio opponitur, quod quidem pertinet ad Romanum Episcopum Episcoporumque coetum. Nemo profecto traditioni fidelis haberi potest qui ligamina nempe recidit ac vincula ab eo eui Christus ipsa in persona Apostoli Petri, ministerium commisit unitatis in Ecclesiam suam.[45]

The root of this schismatic act can be discerned in an incomplete and contradictory notion of Tradition.

Incomplete because it does not take sufficiently into account the *living* character of Tradition, which, as the Second Vatican Council clearly taught, "comes from the apostles and progresses in the Church with the help of the Holy Ghost. There is a growth in insight into the realities and words that are being passed on. This comes about in various ways. It comes through the contemplation and study of believers who ponder these things in their hearts. It comes from the intimate sense of spiritual realities which they experience. And it comes from the preaching of those who have received, along with their right of succession in the episcopate, the sure charism of truth." But especially contradictory is a notion of Tradition which opposes the universal Magisterium of the Church possessed by the Bishop of Rome and the body of bishops. It is impossible to remain faithful to the Tradition while breaking the ecclesial bond with Him whom, in the person of the Apostle Peter, Christ Himself entrusted the ministry of unity in His Church.[46]

45 Note, *Lo Scisma Di Lefebvre,* LXI Apollinaris 529, 547-548 (1988).
46 Joannes Paulus II, *The Apostolic Letter Ecclesia Dei,* Inside the Vatican 20 (Aug./Sept. 1993).

Briefly put, Lefebvre's failure to acknowledge the right-
eousness of the Second Vatican Council is tantamount to
schism.

I. *Ecclesia Dei Afflicta:* The Motu Proprio

After the Vatican's declaration of schism, the motu proprio lays out two rehabilitative steps for those in the Lefebvre
movement:
    1. More liberal and charitable availability of the
Latin Mass
    2. An *Ecclesia Dei* Commission to facilitate full
communion of former followers.

Subsequent to the motu proprio, an *Ecclesia Dei* Commission was established to accomplish these ends:

    1. To allow all those seeking it the use of the
Roman Missal according to the typical edition in
force in 1962, and this in accordance with the norms
already proposed in December 1986, by the Commission of Cardinals instituted for this purpose, having
forewarned this Diocesan Bishop;
    2. a) In accordance with the norm of the motu
proprio *Ecclesia Dei*, to dispense from the irregularities mentioned in canon 1044.1, nn.1 and 2;
        b) To heal in the root marriages celebrated by
these same priests, which are null because of defect
of form as required in canon 1108;
    3. a) To erect the "Priestly Fraternity of Saint
Peter" as a clerical Society of Apostolic Life of Pontifical Right, preserving those particular points made in
n.6a of Apostolic Letter *Ecclesia Dei*, and to approve
the constitutions of the same Society.
        b) Having obtained the consent of the Dioce-
san Bishop, to erect the Seminary of the "Fraternity of
Saint Peter", situated in Wigratzbad in the Diocese of

Augsburg;

4. Canonically to erect as an institute of the consecrated life or as Societies of the Apostolic Life,
communities *de facto* in existence, and which are
bound to the former liturgical and disciplinary forms
of the Latin tradition, after consultation with the
Prefect of the Congregation for Religious and Secular
Institutes;

5. To erect societies of the faithful of the same
mind, which, having undergone a suitable period of
preparation and testing, completed in the customary
way, are potential Institutes of the Consecrated Life
or Societies of the Apostolic Life;

6. Until otherwise provided to exercise the
authority of the Holy See towards these same Societies and Associations.[47]

With the issuance of *Ecclesia Dei Afflicta*, the canonical
stage is set. The Church, by and through its appropriate
authorities, promulgates terms and conditions as to the Latin
Mass, labels "schismatic" the followers of Marcel Lefebvre,
and makes general recommendations as to the "wide and
generous application" of liturgical services to those yet attached to the Tridentine Liturgy "and respect shown for those
with rightful aspirations".

As of this work's publication date, no further formal
action regarding the Archbishop has taken place. With the
Archbishop explained and his actions unraveled, these questions arise. Is the ordination of a bishop, without papal
mandate, an offense triggering automatic (*latae sententiae*)
excommunication? Are there circumstances or extenuating
circumstances that mitigate or provide excusable rationales

---

47 Augustine Card. Mayer *Rescript for Pontifical Commission*, "*Ecclesia Dei*", 77
Canon Law Society, Great Britain & Ireland Newsletter 19, 19-20 (1989).

for the allegation? What defenses are available to one who is accused of ecclesiastical crimes involving the unauthorized consecration of bishops or other schismatic acts? Is disobedience, in every form, always logically, evidence of schism? In summation, . . .are there possible defenses in the case of Marcel Lefebvre, that either excuse the offenses alleged or mitigate the imposed sanctions or penalties? Or is the action of consecration one of strict, undeniable liability? Consideration of these and other juridical issues follows.

CHAPTER 3

The Canonical Background:

The Act of Consecration Without Papal Mandate

On its face, it seems ludicrous to argue that the consecration of a bishop without papal mandate is not punishable. In both the 1917 and 1983 *Codes of Canon Law*, the *Act* is listed as a basis for either *suspension* or excommunication *latae sententiae*. In either case, the delineation seems so *prima facie*. A *latae sententiae* penalty occurs "if a determinate penalty is so attached to the law or precept that it is incurred *ipso facto* upon commission of the crime." [48]

There are a variety of *latae sententiae* impositions in both the 1917 and 1983 Code, though the 1983 version has cut substantially back on the listing. *Latae Sententiae* penalties are either *reserved* to the ordinary or most *specially, specially* or *simply* reserved to the Holy See. Bouscaren, Ellis and Kroth fashioned a complete chart on excommunications *latae sententiae* under the 1917 Code. Notice that unlawful consecrations are not in the excommunication category but under the title *Suspensions*. See *Appendix B*.

---

48 T. Lincoln Bouscaren, Adam C. Ellis, & Francis N. Kroth, Canon Law: A Text and Commentary, 873 (1966).

In the 1917 Code, the unlawful consecration was met with suspension *latae sententiae* and was most specially reserved to the Holy See:

Suspensionem S. Sedi reservatam sententiae.

Episcopus aliquem *consecrans in episcopum* vel loco episcoporum, presbyteri assistentes et qui consecrationem recipit *sine apostolico mandato* contra praescriptum Canon 953, ipso jure suspensi sunt donec Sedes Apostolica eos dispensacerit.[49]

A bishop who consecrates another bishop, the assistant bishops, or the priests who in place of the assistant bishops assist the consecrator, and the newly consecrated bishop who receives consecration without an Apostolic mandate in violation of the precept of Canon 953, are all automatically suspended until the Apostolic See shall have relieved them from the penalty.[50]

Canon 953 in the 1917 Code made plain that no bishop could be ordained except by papal mandate:

Consecratio episcopalis reservatur Romano Pontifici ita ut nulli Episcopo liceat quemquam consecrare in Episcopum, nisi prius constet de pontificio mandato.[51]

The episcopal consecration is reserved to the Roman Pontiff in such a manner that no bishop is allowed to confer episcopal consecration on anyone unless he has first ascertained that there is a papal mandate to that effect.[52]

On April 9, 1951, the Vatican upgraded the suspension penalty to an excommunication:

A Bishop, of whatsoever rite or dignity, who consecrates to the Episcopacy anyone who is neither appointed nor expressly confirmed by the Holy See

---

49 Code of Canon Law, Canon 2370 (1917).
50 Stanislaus Woywod, A Practical Commentary of the Code of Canon Law 558 (1952).
51 Code of Canon Law, Canon 953 (1917.
52 Stanislaus Woywod, A Practical Commentary of the Code of Canon Law 561 (1952).

. . .incurs ipso facto an excommunication *most specially* reserved to the Holy See.[53]

The 1983 Code continues the *latae sententiae* excommunication for the unlawful consecration of a bishop. At Canon 1013 the policy is espoused:

Canon 1013 - Nulli Episcopo licet quemquam consecrare in Episcopum, nisi prius constet de pontificio mandato.[54]

Canon 1013 - No bishop is permitted to consecrate anyone a bishop unless it is first evident that there is a pontifical mandate.[55]

The remedial step taken for unauthorized consecration is posed at Canon 1382:

Canon 1382 - Episcopus qui sine pontificio mandato aliquem consecrat in Episcopum, itemque qui ab eo consecrationem recipit, in excommonicationem latae sententiae Sedi Apostolicae reservatam incurrunt.[56]

A bishop who consecrates someone a bishop and the person who receives such a consecration from a bishop without pontifical mandate incurs an automatic (*latae sententiae*) excommunication reserved to the Apostolic See.[57]

James A. Coriden, Thomas J. Green & Donald E. Heintschel in their treatise, *Code of Canon Law: A Text and Commentary* note the significance of Canon 1382 being one of the few *latae sententiae* excommunications left when compared to the 1917 Code.

The seriousness of this violation is evident from the fact that it warrants one of only five excommunications reserved to the Holy See. The present canon reflects the ecclesiatical significance of the episcopal

53 Acta Apostolicae Sedia 43-217 Holy Office Decree April 9, 1951.
54 Code of Canon Law, Canon 1013 (1983).
55 Code of Canon Law, Canon 1013 (1983).
56 Code of Canon Law, Canon 1382 (1983).
57 Code of Canon Law, Canon 1382 (1983).

office and the importance of the close papal-episco-
pal relationships for orderly church government.[58]

The 1983 code's philosophical approach is one of marked
moderation and pastorality. Canon 1318 urges church offi-
cers, judges and legislators to use caution in dispensing these
penalties:

<table>
<tr>
<td>Canon 1318 - Latae sententiae poenas ne comminetur legislator, nisi forte in singularia quaedam delicta dolosa, quae vel graviori esse possint scandalo vel efficaciter puniri poenis ferendae sententiae non possint; censuras autem, praesertim excommunicationem, ne constituat, nisi maxima cum moderatione et in sola delicta graviora.[59]</td>
<td>Canon 1318 - A legislator is not to threaten automatic penalties (latae sententiae) unless perhaps against certain particularly treacherous offenses which either can result in more serious scandal or cannot be effectively punished by means of inflicted penalties (ferendae sententiae); a legislator is not to establish censures, especially excommunication, except with the greatest moderation and only for more serious offenses.[60]</td>
</tr>
</table>

"Only if a given offense cannot be dealt with
adequately through a *ferendae sententiae* penalty or if
it involves serious scandal, is there room for a particular law *latae sententiae* penalty. It is not clear
precisely what is meant by serious scandal, but it
apparently refers to a situation in which a given
Christian value(s) would be in serious danger of
being taken lightly or violated by members of the
Christian community. While the 1917 Code explic-
itly called for moderation in the use of censures,
especially excommunication, the explicit reference to
moderation in employing *latae sententiae* penalties is
new. The restraint of the revised Code in determining *latae sententiae* penalties (seventeen in present

---

58 James A. Coriden, Thomas J. Green & Donald E. Heintschel, Code of Canon
     Law: A Text and Commentary 925-36 (1990).
59 Code of Canon Law, Canon 1318 (1983).
60 Code of Canon Law, Canon 1318 (1983).

law) and such censures as excommunication (seven in present law) should guide lower-level legislators."[61]

That Archbishop Marcel Lefebvre conducted an unauthorized consecration is not a point of contention. The *Act* was done. But *Acts* are not the sole basis in the determination of ecclesiastical wrongs. An act in and of itself has no moral dimension or inherent imputability. An act must be linked to a mental state, an intent or mindset. Even *latae sententiae* excommunications cannot wrest judgment by the action alone. Both the 1917 and 1983 Code insist on a mental *imputability* to find one liable for the acts they commit. Canonical imputability is fully discussed in Chapter 5. Before finding the Archbishop imputable, some discussion of why sanctions and Church discipline are part of the canonical method is considered.

---

61 James A. Coriden, Thomas J. Green & Donald E. Heintschel, Code of Canon Law: A Text and Commentary 900 (1990).

CHAPTER 4

Church Sanctions and Church Discipline
Under the Codes of Canon Law

I. Canonical Punishment

Critical to this inquiry is the jurisprudence of Church sanctions under both the old and the new *Code of Canon Law*. Why punish anyway? When should sanctions be used? Should non-penal steps be favored over formal penalties? Would Archbishop Marcel Lefebvre be accountable under both Codes (1917 and 1983), or only under the recent version? The queries are essential in the search for imputability and such commentary lays a groundwork for the specific defense issues to follow.

A. The Code of 1917

The 1917 *Code of Canon Law* was exactingly formal when compared to the current 1983 Code. Legalism in the good sense was the underpinning for the 1917 Code, mirroring the age's penchant for authoritarian and hierarchical structure. Even the definitions, terms and descriptions employed approach the Code as an instrument of punishment for the sake of correction rather than correction for the sake of pastorality. Bouscaren, Ellis and Korth support this contention by this description:

An ecclesiastical penalty is a privation of some good for the correction of the culprit and for the punishment of the crime, inflicted by lawful ecclesiastical authority (c. 2215). The good of which the delinquent is deprived must, of course, be one which is under the control of the Church; for example, the sacraments, the right to assist at the Holy Sacrifice, indulgences, the right of patronage, temporal goods, reputation. Grace as such, merit as such are directly in the hands of God; these cannot be *directly* controlled by ecclesiastical penalties. [62]

The 1917 Code classified penalties according to their purposes, and for the most part, the philosophy behind the penalties was not rehabilitative. These penalties were:

1. Poenis medicinalibus seu censuris;	1. Censures (medicinal in design);
2. Poenis vindicativis;	2. Vindictive penalties;
3. Remediis poenalibus et poenitentiis. [63]	3. Penal remedies and reconsiderations. [64]

The promulgation of the *Codex Iuris Canonici* in 1917 marked in that sense a new period with a codified system of laws and, at the same time, a new systematic approach to the laws. The Holy See urged the exegetical and analytical method and discouraged systematic expositions. Presentations of juridical institutions were recommended, for which a genetic historical method was suggested, in order to disclose the origin, development, and charges of the institute as to clarify the presence of the existing norms.[65]

Even with this juridic formalism, the Church authorities cautioned jurists on the application of penalties. The authors

---

62 T. Lincoln Bouscaren, Adam C. Ellis & Francis N. Korth, Canon Law: A Text and Commentary 873 (1966).
63 Code of Canon Law, Canon 2216 (1917).
64 Code of Canon Law, Canon 2216 (1917).
65 Myriam Wiljeus, *Theology and Science of Canon Law: A Historical and Systematic Overview*, 16 Lourain Studies 292, 299-300 (1991).

of Canon 2214.2 of the 1917 Code promoted a passionate, empathetic approach despite the formalism:

> Bishops and other Ordinaries should remember that they are shepherds and not slave-drivers, and that they must rule over their subjects as not to domineer over them but to love them as sons and brothers; they should endeavor by exhortation and admonition to deter them from wrongdoing lest they be obliged to administrate due punishment after faults have been committed. Yet if through human frailty their subjects do wrong, they must observe the precept of the Apostles, and reprove, entreat, rebuke them in all patience and doctrine; for sympathy is often more effective for correction than severity, exhortation better than threats of punishments, kindness better than insistence on authority. If in view of the seriousness of a crime there be need of punishment, then they most combine authority with leniency, judgment with mercy, severity with moderation, to the end that discipline, so salutary and essential to public order, be maintained without asperity, and that those who have been punished may amend their ways, or if they refuse to do so, that others may be deterred from wrongdoing by the salutary example of their punishment. [66]

Under the 1917 *Code of Canon Law*, extenuating circumstances and other defensive rationales could be successfully advocated though their pertinence to individual situations was more rigidly interpreted. A summary of the Code's exemptions from liability is:

---

66 Jose L. Bernacer, Sanctions in the Church, Reading, Cases, Materials in Canon Law: A Text for Ministerial Students 440 (Jordan F. Hite & Daniel J. Ward, ed., 1990).

1. Whatever excuses from mortal guilt excuses from all penalties (c. 2218, §2).

2. From penalties *latae sententiae*, if the law has special expressions, any diminution of imputability on the part of the intellect or the will excuses (c. 2229, §2).

3. Ignorance, neither affected, nor crass, excuses from medicinal but not from vindictive penalties, even though the law has not the special expressions (c. 2229, §3, 1°).

4. Grave fear (not necessarily unjust and external) excuses from penalties *latae sententiae* even if the act was intrinsically wrong and gravely culpable, but not if it tends to the contempt of the faith or of ecclesiastical authority or to the public harm of souls (c. 2229, §3, 3°).

5. Persons before puberty are exempt from *latae sententiae* penalties, but their accomplices incur them (c. 2230); this exemption probably applies to girls up to 14.

6. Unless named, Cardinals are exempt from all penal laws, Bishops from suspension and interdict *latae sententiae*, but not from excommunication (c. 2227). Princes or rulers and their children or proximate expectant successors, Cardinals, and Bishops, even titular, and Papal Legates are exempt form all penalties except those inflicted or declared by the Roman Pontiff (c. 2227). [67]

There is little question that the Archbishop's unauthorized consecration was arguably defensible under the 1917 Code, though the burden was much more arduous than under the present Code.

---

67 T. Lincoln Bouscaren, Adam C. Ellis & Francis N. Korth, Canon Law: A Text and Commentary 881-82 (1966).

A new Code, that of 1983, is the legislation that controls our analysis. Even the most inexperienced reader and interpreter will soon discern the *novus habitus mentis* of the 1983 model.

B. The Code of 1983

Canonists and scholars have little reservation about the metamorphosis of the 1917 Code after Vatican II. Proponents of the New Code were antagonistic of the old, juridical way of accomplishing discipline in the Church. Instead, they proposed a new "spirit of the new canons." [68]

To others, the Code should complement the new mind, the novel way of thinking or mindset of the church since Vatican II. Canonist Elizabeth McDonough, O. P., labels this canonical advance the *novus habitus mentis.* [69]

Most significantly, the 1983 Code resists the application of sanctions. McDonough urges that sanctions be used as a last resort.

Concern for reform of offenders and for reparation of scandal or harm, along with concern for protection of a person's reputation, appears consistently in the canons on sanctions as well as in other parts of the revised code. In particular, the first canon in the title on application of penalties employs the two standard elements of the rationale for penal law and combines them with a third, related element to express what could be called the "Three R's" for the canon law of sanctions. The "Three R's" contained in Canon 1341 are: reform of the offender, restoration of justice, and reparation of scandal. They appear

68 Jordan F. Hite, Readings, Cases, Materials in Canon Law: A Textbook for Ministerial Studies (1990).
69 Elizabeth McDonough, *A Novus Habitus Mentis For Sanctions in the Church*, 48 The Jurist 727 (1988).

there as the goals to be sought whenever a competent ordinary must decide whether to proceed with a penal process. Moreover, the ordinary is enjoined by the canon to initiate the process for application of any penalty only after he has ascertained that these "Three R's" cannot be sufficiently achieved by other means. [70]

Aside from this rehabilitative interest, the Code is adverse to presumed imputability. The new mindset of the Code should eliminate any presumption of malicious intent or *dolus*. McDonough highlights these new features most intelligently:

> [A] person is not liable to a penalty when the offense is imputable through *culpa* unless the law or precept specifically states this. . . [71]

Canon 1317 of the 1983 Code emphasizes this hesitancy towards the establishment of penal solutions in disciplinary situations:

Canon 1317 - Poenae eatenus constituantur, quatenus vere necessariae sint ad aptius providendum ecclesiasticae disciplinae. Dimissio autem e statu clericali lege particulari constitui nequit. [72]

Canon 1317 - Penalties should be established to the extent to which they are truly necessary to provide more suitably for ecclesiastical discipline. Dismissal from the clerical state, however, cannot be established by particular law. [73]

Penalties under the 1983 Code are to be used only when *vere necessaria*. Coriden, Green and Heintschel address this reticence in the 1983 Code.

---

70 Elizabeth McDonough, *A Novus Habitus Mentis for Sanctions in the Church*, 48 The Jurist 727, 729-30 (1988).
71 Elizabeth McDonough, *A Novus Habitus Mentis for Sanctions in the Church*, 48 The Jurist 727, 732 (1988).
72 Code of Canon Law, Canon 1317 (1983).
73 Code of Canon Law, Canon 1317 (1983).

The current emphasis on penalties as a last resort in coping with pastoral problems is evident in this admonition to infra-universal legislators to establish penalties only in instances in which it is absolutely necessary to provide appropriately for the exigencies of ecclesiastical discipline. There is a concern to mitigate possibly excessive episcopal penal initiatives here.... This is a wise causation inasmuch as the sharp reduction in penalties for specific offenses in the revised Code might tempt other legislators to multiply such penalties in particular law. [74]

Additionally, supportive of this non-penal direction in the 1983 Code are Canons 1318 and 1319. Canon 1318, cited previously, directs jurists and legislators to use *caution* in the application of any *latae sententiae* penalties. Canon 1319, while affording disciplinary authority at §1, uses words of restriction at §2.

Canon 1319 - §1. Quatenus quis potest vi potestatis regiminis in foro externo praecepta imponere, eatenus potest etiam poenas determinatas, exceptis expiatoriis perpetuis, per praeceptum comminari. §2 Praeceptum peonale ne feratur, nisi re mature perpensa, et iis servatis, quae in cann. 1317 et 1318 de legibus particularibus statuuntur. [75]	Canon 1319 - §1. To the extent that one can impose precepts in the external forum by virtue of the power of governance, to that same extent one can also threaten determinate penalties through a precept with the exception of perpetual expiatory penalties. §2 A penal precept is not to be issued without a mature consideration of the matter and without observing what is stated in Canon 1317 and 1318 concerning particular laws. [76]

---

74 James A. Coriden, Thomas J. Green & Donald E. Heintschel, Code of Canon Law: A Text and Commentary 899 (1990).
75 Code of Canon Law, Canon 1319 (1983).
76 Code of Canon Law, Canon 1319 (1983).

The tenor of these Canons indicates that only in the gravest of cases will penalties be applied. Coriden, Green and Heintshel confirm this philosophy:

The serious implications of such penalties make it imperative that they not be employed lightly but rather that they be implemented only through the strict procedures of law. [77]

Dejuridizing the 1917 Code is a fundamental premise of the 1983 Code. Instead of commands and ultimatums, instead of the systematic and punishment response mechanisms, the authors of the 1983 Code hope for an approach based on the Christian community. *Imperium* was replaced by "communio". Stated another way, the mind of the Council (Vatican II) was to be infused into canonical precepts. Pope Paul VI so spoke:

Canon law is the law of a society that is indeed visible but also supernatural; a society which is built up through the Word and the sacraments, and whose objective is to lead people to eternal salvation. For this reason, it is a sacred law, entirely distinct from civil law. It is a law of a very special, hierarchical nature, and proceeds from the very will of Christ. It is totally incorporated in the salvific action of the Church, by which She continues the work of Redemption. By its very nature, then, canon law is *pastoral*. It is an expression and instrument of the *apostolic function*, and a constitutive element of the Church of the Incarnate Word [78]

77 James A. Coriden, Thomas J. Green & Donald E. Heintschel, Code of Canon Law: A Text and Commentary 900 (1990).
78 Paul VI, Allocation to the Sacred Roman Rota, 8 February 1973, AAS 65 (1973): 96 (English translation: "The Value of Canonical Equity," The Pope Speaks 18 (1973-1974: 76).

Law is not necessarily and solely the work of canonists and primates, but more so a reflection of the *spirit* of the Church:

> The end of the law, besides the good of the community, is the protection of the autonomy of the person in the Christian existence. Justice is a returning point in his teaching [79]

Pope John Paul II poses a similar line of support for the 1983 Code in *Sacrae disciplinae leges.* [80]
Law is not solely coercion or juridical remedy. The Code must mirror image faith, grace, charity and the charisms of the Church. The Pontiff related in 1983:

> [I]ts purpose is rather to create such an order in the ecclesial society that, while assigning primacy to love, grace, and charisma, it at the same time renders their organic development easier in the life of both the ecclesial society and the individual persons belonging to it. [81]

All in all, the rule of command *(imperium)* was inadequate in light of the Council. John Paul II continues:

> The instrument, which the Code is, fully corresponds to the nature of the Church, especially as it is proposed by the teaching of the Second Vatican Council in general and in a particular way by its ecclesiological teaching. Indeed, in a certain sense this new Code could be understood as a great effort to translate this same conciliar doctrine and ecclesi-

---

79 Myriam Wiljens, Theology and Canon Law, 16 (1992).
80 John Paul II, Apostolic Constitution, "Sacrae disciplinae leges," AAS 75 (1983).
81 John Paul II, Apostolic Constitution, "Sacrae disciplinae leges," AAS 75 (1983).

ology into *canonical* language. If, however, it is impossible to translate perfectly into *canonical* language the conciliar image of the Church, nevertheless the Code must always be referred to this image as the primary pattern whose outline the Code ought to express insofar as it can by its very nature. [82]

In essence, the 1917 Code, according to its opponents, was outdated in light of Church reforms and badly in need of revision. In 1967, A Synod of Bishops approved unanimously an adjusted philosophical approach to the once perceived rigidity of the 1917 Code.

The Bishops remarked:

> To foster the pastoral care of souls as much as possible, the new law, besides the virtue of justice, is to take cognizance of charity, temperance, humaneness and moderation, whereby equity is to be pursued not only in the application of the laws by pastors of souls but also in the legislation itself. Hence, unduly rigid norms are to be set aside and rather recourse is to be taken to exhortations and persuasions where there is no need of a strict observance of the law on account of the public good and general ecclesiastical discipline. [83]

Put another way, let's not get hung up on law as the singular means in disciplinary cases. Employ the law only when other remedial steps have failed. Use the law as a last resort! Canonist Ladislas Orsy labels the 1983 Code, when compared to the 1917 Code, a completely *New Method*. He synthesizes the method of the 1983 Code.

---

82 Code of Canon Law: Latin-English Version, xiv (1983).
83 Code of Canon Law: Latin-English Version, xx - xxi (1983).

• *The movement from imperium to communio* was made possible by the immense progress before the Council in historical research which brought into the forefront the ancient idea and practice of *communio*. From a higher viewpoint, *imperium* lost its attraction.

• *The change from confessional conflict to ecumenical understanding* was facilitated by a fresh look at all the Christian churches and communities. While earlier observers saw in them nothing but abomination, the Council perceived among them the signs of God's grace in the presence of the Word and the sacraments they possessed. From that higher perspective, the mutual relationships between them and the Roman Catholic community appeared differently. Thus, the heretics and schismatics became our brothers and sisters.

• Similarly, *the move from defensive isolation to an appreciation of secular values* and to a more direct service of the human family could happen only because the Council fathers came to a better perception of the goodness of all things in this creation and of the dignity of every human person in it. From contemplating our whole planet and listening to the cry of the needy everywhere, they came to a much better understanding of the mission of the church.

• Also, *the Council moved away from a philosophy that could think in static categories only.* Inspired by the discoveries of empirical sciences and informed by historical data, the fathers accepted a developmental view of the universe. This new stance helped them to reach a better understanding of how the word of God keeps developing in our midst without ever losing its original meaning. [84]

In the 1983 Code, infractions are remedied not by order or demand, but by an insistence that rejection from the Christian community *(communio)* is satisfactory. The notion

84 Ladislas Orsy, Theology and Canon Law: New Horizons for Legislation and Interpretation 15 (1992).

that *communio* replaced imperium is telling. Instead of retribution, the Church, by the use of excommunication, hopes the penalty moves you appropriately, bends you in the right shapes, leads you back to the community to which you belong. Canonist Von Stephen Kotzula's comprehensive work, *Zur Exkommunikation im CIC/1983*, portrays the modern Code's views of *communio* and its interralationship with excommunication:

Die Exkommunikation stellt diejenige Beugestrafe des kanonischen Rechtes dar, welche die Katholische Kirche ob ihres Selbstzeugnisses willen gleichsam als *ultima ration* rechtens verfügt, wodursh Sie, ohne die Teilhabe an ihren geistlichen Gütern vollends zu verweigern, die Rechstfähigkeit am umfangreichsten mindert, ja diese nach verhängter Spruchstrafe bzw. nach ergangenem Feststellungsurteil für die aktive Ausübung sogar entzieht, um auf diese Weise das Wohl der Communio zu gewährleisten und dem Straftäter nach sichtlicher Sinnesänderung den Neuzugang zur Communio wieder vollauf zu ermöglichen. [85]

The excommunication represents the "bending punishment" of the canon law, which the Catholic Church has at her disposal as *ultima ratio*, throught which She, without totally refusing the partaking of her spiritual goods, diminishes the corporate capacity to the largest extent possible, indeed after judgment has been pronounced, takes away the active practice, in order to ensure the good of the Communio, and to enable the "criminal" after having shown a change of mind, to again fully enter into the community. [86]

For the Vatican, the *bend* hasn't accomplished its end. In the 1983 Code, understanding replaced apologetics thereby making "heretics and schismatics our brothers." [87]

In the 1983 Code, secularism was welcomed, behavioral sciences elevated and the world, as the world is, considered essential to any honest, canonical inquiry.

85 Stephen Kotzula, *Zur Exkommunikation im CIC/1983*, Archiv Für Katholisches Kirchenrecht 432, 459 (Jan. 1987).
86 Stephen Kotzula, *Zur Exkommunikation im CIC/1983*, Archiv Für Katholisches Kirchenrecht 432, 459 (Jan. 1987).
87 Ladislas Orsy, Theology and Canon Law: New Horizons for Legislation and Interpretation 15 (1992).

Undeniably, the 1983 Code's method is what Archbishop Marcel Lefebvre abhors. Making welcome those who deny Rome's authority, unifying the world into the Church, putting non-theological sciences on par with canonical and theological studies, are all signs of the Church faltering. Yet, this is the same Code that hammered him; the same Code that bludgeoned home the unacceptability of holding fast to Tradition as he knew it; the same Code that excommunicated a man who never once disagreed with dogma, doctrine or any essential Church teachings, and who always upheld the Papacy. By any standard, there was little effort to understand, even ecumenically, the Archbishop. Command *(imperium)* was the only means employed on the resolution of the case. Myriam Wiljens sees the Code of 1983 as evidence of the Church's decision to enter the world. Rather than exhibiting the historical pattern of *defensive isolation,* the Church welcomed the world in. She states effectively:

> They took a fresh look at all the churches and communities. (c) With Trent, the Church moved into a defensive isolated position. At Vatican II, the bishops got a better view of the whole planet. This led to an appreciation of secular values, and also they perceived the cry of the needy. (d) The discoveries of the empirical sciences, together with new world historical insights allowed the Fathers to move away from a static world view to a dynamic one. [88]

But is the action of the Church against Marcel Lefebvre a symbol of this just developed dynamism — of a Church willing to deal with the "New." Or is the penalty chosen selectively reserved to those in the Church exhibiting a conservative bent? If the 1983 Code supposedly broke with the

---

88 Myriam Wiljens, Theology and the Science of Canon Law: A Historic and Systematic Overview, 16 Lourain Studies 292, 303 (1991).

rigidity of the past, affording a more flexible design in the resolution of dilemmas, how can the Church explain its juridical actions against Marcel Lefebvre? Michael Novak's critical commentary on Vatican II, *The Open Church*, recounts the philosophical shift in what "Church" meant during preliminary Council discussions. The hierarchical, bureaucratical-tiered Church was static and outmoded for modern life. The Church is instead, its *people!* Novak highlights the discussion:

> Gregory VII tried to free the Church from temporal power by building up a juridical system based upon the rights of the hierarchy; the laity was made to become more and more passive in the Church. "But a new era has arrived." The term "people of God," becoming so popular in this session, is "as old as Abraham." [89]

In this light, the canonical penalties imposed on Marcel Lefebvre are ironic. The revisionist underpinning of the 1983 Code is the elimination of the penal canonist Edwards N. Peters' 1991 dissertation surveys the emphasis on dejuridizing the Code:

> There was, it seems, a veritable chorus of calls for penal law reform both before and after Vatican II. The desire for a major simplification of both substantive and procedural penal law grew out of the recognition that the *ius vigens* then was too complex to be practiced effectively, and instead was falling into desuetude.
>
> In general, it seems that penal reform sought not simply to improve the technical language and structure of the law for its own sake, but also to respond

89 Michael Novak, The Open Church, Vatican II, Act II, 93 (1964).

to the demands for increased accountability to the faithful in general and victims of alleged injustice in particular. There was a recognized need to evidence impartiality on the part of ecclesiastical authority in the administration of justice. [90]

Openness, *communio*, secularism in the Church, and the *novus habitus mentis* of the 1983 Code should afford a punishment alternative to Marcel Lefebvre. Esteemed canonist Neri Capponi expresses enlightened bafflement on Lefebvre's *latae sententiae* excommunication:

The extenuating circumstances are — there's a list of them in the code, one more lenient that the other. Their practical effect is that ninety-nine times out of a hundred the penalty does not apply. It's ridiculous, perfectly ridiculous. [91]

Therefore, at least guided by the new philosophical approach of the 1983, and its aversion to penalties, it appears juridically unsound that Archbishop Marcel Lefebvre was *latae sententiae* excommunicated and declared a schismatic.

The analysis now turns to specific defense considerations.

90 Edward N. Peters, Penal Procedural Law in the 1983 Code of Canon Law, 355 (1991).
91 Note, *Church Law, Jargon, Free and Interview with Count Neri Capponi*, 2 *Latin Mass Magazine* 14, 16 (May-June 1993).

CHAPTER 5

Imputability

LEGAL ISSUE #1: Whether imputability can be discerned or determined solely from the action of Archbishop Marcel Lefebvre?

I. The Nature of Imputability

Imputability is the subjective element in any alleged violation or delict:[92]

> "Imputability, therefore, denotes a relationship between an agent and his act. It is a causal relationship of a particular kind. Mere physical causality is not enough to establish imputability; it must be a relationship of moral causality. Responsibility, on the other hand, bespeaks a relationship between the agent and some third party. Thus, a crime is imputable to the delinquent, but the delinquent is responsible to society. In penal law, responsibility is the opposite of excuse for penalty; and it means that the delinquent is answerable to society and must, therefore, pay the penalty imposed by law."[93]

---

92 Elizabeth McDonough, *Novus Habitus Mentis for Sanctions in the Church*, 48 The Jurist 727, 738 (1988).
93 Robert Swoboda, Ignorance in Relation to the Imputability of Delicts, Innocent 88 (1941).

Free will and *scientia* (knowledge) of the act is the basis for imputing ecclesiastical crimes.[94]

"Two elements are necessarily involved in imputability, namely, deliberation and free will. Crime, as every violation of law, is formally constituted by the will. It is the free volition of the delinquent which is the cause of crime. This is frequently brought out in the terminology of the legal texts, in which the subjective element or imputability is called *animus* or *voluntas*, or is qualified by the word *sponte* and other similar expressions, which will be discussed below in the consideration of *dolus*."[95]

A. Imputability Under the Code of 1917

In the 1917 Code a delict or ecclesiastical crime was defined as:

Canon 2195 - §1. Nomine delicti, iure ecclesiastico, intelligitur externa et moraliter imputabilis legis violatio, cui addita sit sanctio canonica saltem indeterminata.[96]	In Canon Law, the term "offense" implies an external and morally imputable violation of a law, to which at least an indeterminate canonical sanction is attached.[97]

Under the 1917 Code an external violation *(externa. . . violatio)* was insufficient without moral imputability *(moralitea imputabilis)*. The violation had to be codified under a specific law or precept with a canonical sanction. The measure of moral imputability is grounded in a dual formula:

1. The act was committed with malice *(dolus)*

---

94 John J. McGrath, Comparative Study of Crime and its Imputability in Ecclesiastical Criminal Law and in American Criminal Law, 46 (1957).
95 Robert Swoboda, Ignorance in Relation to the Imputability of Delicts, Innocent 88 (1941).
96 Code of Canon Law, Canon 2195 §1 (1917).
97 Stanislaus Woywod, A Practical Commentary on the Code of Canon Law 447 (1957).

2. The act was committed in ignorance or an omission of due diligence *(culpa)*

Both *dolus* and *culpa* signify degrees of imputability. Dolus is the deliberate, malicious intention to breach a law. Culpa is the failure to do or act when responsible to do so - a sort of negligence by omission.

Canon 2200 §1 at the 1917 Code defines intent as a *voluntas violandi legem*.[98] Will, the choice to do the act, is the result of some conceived deliberation. On its face, the actions of Marcel Lefebvre, of June 30, 1988 manifest deliberation and free choice.

1. Intent, Malice, Dolus Under the 1917 Code

Canonists have expended considerable energy distinguishing *dolus* by its two defined forms: either *simple* or *perfect*. In the case of simple *dolus* the intention in violating the law might be based on defective knowledge or intent.

On the other hand, *perfect dolus* means complete, inerrant and unequivocal knowledge of the wrong done. "The evil will *(dolus)*, spoken of in Canon 2199, means a deliberate will to violate a law, and presupposes on the part of the mind a knowledge of the law and on the part of the will freedom of action."[99] Canon 2229 at §2 holds in the absence of full and ordered knowledge, no penalty will apply. In a case of *perfect dolus*, the charged party must have *scienter*, be *praesumpseria*, or *consulto egerit*. This distinction is more than academic.

"This distinction is of importance in understanding the legal principles regarding the effects of fear upon responsi-

---

98 Code of Canon Law, Canon 2200 §1 (1917).
99 Stanislaus Woywod, A Practical Commentary on the Code of Canon Law 450 (1952).

bility, and a proper knowledge of this distinction is especially necessary for the practical application of these principles to individual laws."[100]

Under the 1917 Code at Canon 2370, the provision dealing with unauthorized consecration, *perfect dolus* language is not apparent. Canon 2370 lists the action of consecration with no reference to mental states. This being the case, at least under the 1917 Code, the malice required by the Archbishop would be *simple* in nature. Simple *dolus* in the consecration of the bishops would be sufficient in law raising the presumption of intent.

Assume *arguendo* that the Archbishop met the requirement of simple *dolus*, a plain intent to violate Canon 2370 (1917) as to the unauthorized consecration of a bishop. The 1917 Code affords those charged with defenses based on various exemptions and exceptions. In particular, reference is made to penalties *latae sententiae* which are exempted or at least minimized. Those categories that influence a finding of imputability are:

Age: .... Canon 2204
Mental Disturbance: .... Canon 2201
Drinking, Drugs, Sloth: .... Canon 2201 (3)
Ignorance/Mistake: .... Canon 2202 (1)
Uncontrollable Events: .... Canon 2203 (2)
Omission of Due Diligence: .... Canon 2203 (1)
Force: .... Canon 2205 (1)
Legitimate Defense or Provocation: .... Canon 2205 (4)
Passion:.............................. Canon 2206
Fear/Hardship/Necessity: .... Canon 2205 (2)

---

100 Alan Edward McCoy, *Force and Fear in Relation to Delictual Imputability and Penal Responsibility*, An Historical Synopsis and Commentary 54, 62 (1944).

When these conditions exist, imputability is mitigated or exorcised. Canon 2201 (1) sets out the general policy on exemption or exceptional circumstances:

Delicti sunt incapaces qui actu carent usu rationis.[101]	Persons who actually do not enjoy the use of reason are incapable of committing an offense.[102]

Of all the Archbishop's extenuating circumstances, a defense of fear/hardship and necessity has meritorious possibilities. That consideration will occur in Chapter 7. Therefore, as a general policy, under the Code of 1917, the Archbishop's *latae sententiae* penalty of excommunication, while automatic by the consecration itself, based on simple *dolus*, can be defended, excused or mitigated if a case of fear/hardship or necessity is demonstrated. This canonical principle recognizes that other legal or factual conditions may disallow the defenses. A full discussion of these possibilities will occur *supra*.

2. Culpa and Imputability Under the 1917 Code

The second basis in a finding of imputability is *culpa*. *Culpa* is generally defined as an omission or a failure "to exercise due care, which will generally consist in a culpable failure to foresee the injurious effects of an action. The formal note of culpa as a souce of delictural liability is the morally imputable absence of due care or negligence. The basis of culpa is therefore moral guilt.[103]

The 1917 Code has a prophetic quality to it, asking the actor to understand the consequences of action, labelling the omission a lack of due care and diligence in estimating future

---

101 Code of Canon Law, Canon 2201 §1 (1917).
102 Stanislaus Woywod, A Practical Commentary on the Code of Canon Law 451 (1952).
103 Robert Swoboda, Ignorance in Relation to the Imputability of Delicts, Innocent 103 (1941).

results "*omissionem debisae diligentiae in asetimandis effectibus facilez*".[104]

Culpa, in the most general sense, means voluntary neglect often synonymously termed *neglectus, negligentia,* and *inperitia.* There are varying degrees of *culpa* from *latae, levis* to *levissima.* When compared to *dolus, culpa* has less of an intentional flavor. "[T]he effect is either foreseen but nevertheless culpably permitted because of a failure in the duty to prevent a foreseen criminal result; or the effect is due to negligence in not forseeing the violation of the law."[105] "In other words, in a *delictum culposum* the criminal deed is not directly willed, but is the morally imputable result of a voluntary action. It matters not whether the voluntary act from which the delictual fact results be in itself licit or illicit."[106]

In this sense, a culpa is either an omission or commission regarding a failure to exercise due care. Foreseeability as to one's responsibility plays a role in determining *culpa.* In addition, the party supposedly delict must have a duty to others.[107]

Guided by the Code of 1917, the action of Archbishop Marcel Lefebvre may provide a basis for imputability under a theory of *culpa.* The commission of unauthorized consecrations clearly had ramifications. In *culpa* analysis, it is the negligence, the disregard — not the malice that dictates imputability. If the Archbishop had not the power or the capacity to ordain, the question of *culpa* would be irrelevant. "Thus, there is no duty to foresee an effect, whose very

104 Code of Canon Law, Canon 2200 (1917).
105 Alan Edward McCoy, *Force and Fear in Relation to Delictual Imputabaility and Penal Responsibility,* An Historical Synopsis and Commentary 54, 70 (1944).
106 Robert Swoboda, Ignorance in Relation to the Imputability of Delicts, Innocent 102 (1941).
107 Robert Swoboda, Ignorance in Relation to the Imputability of Delicts, Innocent 106 (1941).

existence and possibility is not so much as suspected, and hence there can be no *culpa* in such an absence of foresight."[108]

However, in the case before us, any reasonable interpreter must conclude, that foresight was plainly envisioned. In summary, then, according to the 1917 Code imputability resulted from either *dolus* or *culpa* (c. 2199), while *dolus* required a deliberate intention to violate the law and could be defective either in knowledge or in violation or both (c. 2200, §1). The use of certain legal terminology exempted one from (some) automatic penalties if full knowledge and deliberation were not present (c. 2229, §2). Yet, subsequent to an external violation, the law presumed one had acted with *dolus* (a deliberate intention to violate) and contrary proof was required to overturn the presumption (c. 2200, §2).[109]

3. Imputability Under the Code of 1983

If the Archbishop can pose defenses under the Code of 1917, his opportunities for defense are greatly expanded under the 1983 Code. More specifically, Canon 1321 limits generically imputability in this narrow fashion.

Can. 1321 - §1. Nemo punitur, nisi externa legis vel praecepti violatio, ab eo commissa, sit graviter imputabilis ex dolo vel ex culpa.	Can. 1321 - §1. No one is punished unless the external violation of the law or a precept committed by the person is seriously imputable to that person by reason of malice or culpability.

---

108 Robert Swoboda, Ignorance in Relation to the Imputabaility of Delicts, Innocent 106 (1941).
109 Elizabeth McDonough, *A Gloss on Canon 1321*, 21 Studia Canonica, 381, 386 (1987).

§2. Poena lege vel praecepto statuta is tenetur, qui legem vel praeceptum deliberate violavit; qui vero id egit
ex omissione debitae diligentiae, nor
punitur, nisi lex vel praeceptum aliter
caveat.

§3. Posita externa violatione, im-
putabilitas praesumitur, nisi aliud appareat.[110]

§2. A person who has deliberately violated a law or a precept is
bound by the penalty stated in that
law or that precept; unless a law or a
precept provides otherwise, a person who has violated that law or that
precept through a lack of necessary
diligence is not punished.

§3 Unless it is otherwise evident, imputability is presumed
whenever an external violation has
occurred.[111]

While it is still a presumed violation when an external
violation occurs, the Code of 1983 varies both in tone and
terminology as to the validity of the presumption. Imputability is presumed "unless it is otherwise evident" or "*nisi
aliud appareat*"[112] otherwise in the 1983 Code. In 1917, the
party under penalty was required to "*prove*"[113] otherwise.

B. The Disappearance of Dolus

The consequences of the new Canon 1321, §3 may be in
inverse proportion to the amount of discussion it has received. "No mention of either the *dolus/imputabilitias* or the
probetur/appareat change appears in reports of the meetings
subsequent to circulation of the 1973 schema or in the 1981
Relatio. The only comments about §3 were made in the
Praenotanda of the 1973 schema where it was simply noted in
one sentence that the presumption of imputability ceased not
only from contrary proof but as often as it appeared otherwise. Another sentence explained that the former presumption of *dolus* had been suppressed because the canonical
notion of *dolus* includes an intention to violate the law and
that, although a presumption could be made regarding the

---

110 Code of Canon Law, Canon 1321 (1983).
111 Code of Canon Law, Canon 1321 (1983).
112 Code of Canon Law, Canon 1321, §3 (1983).
113 Code of Canon Law, Canon 2200 §2 (1917).

intention to place or to omit an action, a presumption about an intention to violate the law seemed less reasonable."[114]

The practical implication for any evidentiary burden is obvious. Any canonical inquiry of the Archbishop must weigh by his life, his actions, his mind and intent, and could argue that he lacked *dolus* (malice) despite any external violation by the consecrations. If the presumption of the violation is eliminated in the 1983 Code, the external violation is not sufficient, in and of itself. The 1983 Code describes *dolus* in finding imputability "as the deliberate will to violate a law or precept. None of the proposed canons provided specific legal words or phases without which one was not liable to *latae sententiae* penalties, but an earlier canon of the 1973 schema stated that penalties could be incurred automatically only if the law or precept expressly state this consequence. Circumstances that excused, mitigated, or increased liability for penalties were mentioned in subsequent canons."[115]

Thus, the Archbishop, under the Code of 1983, if he shows a lack of malice *(dolus)*, and his action is prompted by fear/hardship and necessity, can challenge the charge of imputability.

C. Culpa and Imputability Under the 1983 Code

As in the 1917 Code, *culpa* provides a secondary avenue for imputability. Canon 1321 at §1 and §2 relates:

114 Elizabeth McDonough, *A Gloss on Canon 1321*, 21 Studia Canonica, 381, 384 (1987).
115 Elizabeth McDonough, *A Gloss on Canon 1321*, 21 Studia Canonica, 381, 386 (1987).

Canon 1321 - §1. Nemo punitur, nisi externa legis vel praecepti violatio, ab eo commissa, sit graviter imputabilis ex dolo vel ex culpa.

§2. Poena lege vel praecepto statuta is tenetur, qui legem vel praeceptum deliberate violavit; qui vero id egit ex omissione debitae diligentiae, nor punitur, nisi lex vel praeceptum aliter caveat.[116]

Canon 1321 - §1. No one is punished unless the external violation of the law or a precept committed by the person is seriously imputable to that person by reason of malice or culpability.

§2. A person who has deliberately violated a law or a precept is bound by the penalty stated in that law or that precept; unless a law or a precept provides otherwise, a person who has violated that law or that precept through a lack of necessary diligence is not punished.[117]

Canonist Elizabeth McDonough sees a striking *culpa* distinction between the Codes of 1917 and 1983 as posed in §2 of Canon 1321:

Three major changes are of importance here, especially as demonstrating the *novus habitus mentis* of the law itself as a transitional stage of change. First, legal imputability does not automatically include malicious intent because it can also arise from negligence or inadvertence. Second, no negligence or inadvertence renders one liable to a sanction unless it has been previously decided and so indicated in the law that a particular offense, when imputable from this cause, will nevertheless be sanctionable. Third, reversing the presumption of imputability after an external violation does not require proof in the strict sense of that term with which canonists are most familiar from marriage cases. In other words there are, in fact, entirely new affirmations in this norm itself, and these affirmations require careful analysis and integration with the basic elements of a delict as contained in the former code as well as a

116 Code of Canon Law, Canon 1321 §§1 & 2 (1983).
117 Code of Canon Law, Canon 1321 §§1 & 2 (1983).

readiness to ascertain and assimilate the aspects that are truly different.[118]

After consideration of the circumstance of the Archbishop Marcel Lefebvre, it is evident that two defenses arise:

1. That the consecration of bishops, even by a person who violated the law through a lack of diligence but by necessitous reasons, is not subject to subsequent penal sanctions.[119]

2. That even if imputability could be founded on culpa, sufficient evidence could rebut the presumption of imputability *(nisi aliud appareat)*.[120]

Ergo, under the Code of 1983, imputability could not be justified by a theory of *culpa* as to the conduct of Archbishop Marcel Lefebvre.

D. Rebutting the Presumption of Imputability

Before any analysis of extenuating or exceptional circumstances, a sound defense strategy will attempt, *ad limine*, to make tenuous any presumption of imputability. The provisions of both the 1917 and 1983 Code proclaim that external action, a violation, gives rise to a presumption of ecclesiastical wrongs. In the New 1321 (3) — "imputability is presumed" unless it *appears* otherwise, and in the old; it must be *proven* otherwise. The weight of the contrary verbs employed is marked. On the one hand, at least under 1917 provisions, the petitioner must demonstrate evidentiary proof that overturns and rebuts the presumption. The 1917 Code advocate had to satisfactorily demonstrate a well-founded, reasonable doubt *(donec contrarium probetur)*. By

---

118 Elizabeth McDonough, *A Novus Habitus Mentis for Sanctions in the Church*, 48 The Jurist 727, 732 (1988).
119 Code of Canon Law, Canon 1321 §2 (1983).
120 Code of Canon Law, Canon 1321 §3 (1983).

contrast, the 1983 Code's liberal employment of the term "appears" grants greater discretion in the interpretation. McDonough labels the modern "appear" as proof of "the absolute possibility of the contrary sanctions in clear certainty, a laid-faced assertion to the contrary will not suffice."[121]

With this evidentiary standard at hand, the party seeking to avoid imputability must raise doubt sufficient enough to overcome the parameters of Canon 1321 §3. Ponder these arguments:

•What if Archbishop Marcel Lefebvre argued that, by his own reliable sources, the Pope announced his intention never to cooperate in the matter of consecrations?

•What if public pressure of numerous souls crying out for traditional Mass and sacraments overwhelmed the Archbishop to move quickly as to the consecrations?

•What if he was given an oral promise to proceed with the consecrations only to have it unjustifiably withdrawn?

The scenarios posed, hypothetical or factual as they may be, serve to tarnish the luster of any external violation. Evidence of these states and circumstances may, could or might meet the evidentiary burden of *nisi aluid appareat* under Canon 1321 §3. Such an emancipated approach would not conflict with the extraordinary remedies and exceptional circumstances that negate imputability discussed in the canons below. Scholarly canonical authority by McDonough carves out the new canonical reality.

---

121 Elizabeth McDonough, *A Habitus Mentis for Sanctions in the Church,* 48 The Jurist 727, 738 (1988).

Nevertheless, rather minimal evidence that the matter is not in fact what it appears to be should suffice to raise the doubt necessary for vitiating moral certitude in penal cases. This is quite consonant with the intent of the revision *coectus* when it reformulated the legal requirements for imputability in direct contrast to those in the former Code.[122]

It would seem the Archbishop did not benefit from this new approach.

LEGAL HOLDING 1.1: That imputability cannot be discerned or determined by a sole or singular examination of the action of Archbishop Marcel Lefebvre. Imputability has both subjective and objective elements under the 1917 and 1983 Codes.

LEGAL HOLDING 1.2: That the act of consecration requires a simple *dolus,* an errant belief that justifies the wrong, making proof of intent an easier burden under both the 1917 and 1983 Codes.

LEGAL HOLDING 1.3: That under the Code of 1917, it might be argued successfully that the Archbishop was imputable under a *culpa* theory, that is, acted negligently in carrying out the consecration.

LEGAL HOLDING 1.4: That under the 1983 Code the external violation alone will not suffice, even under simple *dolus,* if the Archbishop can explain conditions that *nisi aliud appareat.*

---

122 Elizabeth McDonough, *A Novus Habitus Mentis for Sanctions in the Church,* 48 The Jurist 727, 738 (1988).

CHAPTER 6

Exceptions, Exemptions and Extenuating Circumstances as to Imputability

LEGAL ISSUE #2: Could a finding of initial imputability on the part of Archbishop Marcel Lefebvre, be excused, exempted or excepted by extenuating circumstances or conditions?

I.   The Concept of Canonical Excuse or Execution

Despite an initial finding of imputability or at least a judgment that both the action and objective element were necessarily met, could circumstances excuse the finding? To illustrate, accept that the Archbishop performed the consecrations without papal mandate, and then admittedly he knew it was a violation of canonical precepts. At first glance, all that is called for in establishing ecclesiastical criminality has been achieved, that a law exists, an action to violate the law happened and the deliberate, though not necessary perfect, malice *(dolus)* to act accordingly is established. Do these findings unequivocally rule against the Archbishop? Under either the 1917 or 1983 Code, the judgment cannot be unequivocal for both authorities evaluate conduct not only by the acts themselves, but the circumstances that surround the choice to act.

II. Extenuating Circumstances Under the 1917 Code

That which excuses mortal guilt simultaneously excuses the penalties attached. In the case of the Archbishop, his actions imply and his verbal commentary manifest disobedience to the law. While this judgment is tempting, it is too insular.

Surrounding every crime are the particular circumstances. "Some of these circumstances may take away or diminish the imputability of the crime; others may add to the imputability of the crime. If a circumstance changes the very nature of the crime and turns it into another species of crime, the circumstance does not increase the imputability, since this was included in the very definition of the crime itself."[123]

Hence, a crime appears to be, yet these very appearances deceive. Under Canon 2229, various extenuating circumstances that either negate or diminish imputability are covered.

A. Ignorance

First, ignorance, in the legal sense, nullifies a penalty *latae sententiae*. The Code states:

Canon 2229 - §1. A nullis latae sententiae poenis ignorantia affectata sive legis sive solius poenae excusat, licet lex verba de quibus in §2 contineat[124]

Canon 2229 - §1 *Affected* (pretended) ignorance of either the law or of its penalty only does not excuse from any penalties *latae sententiae*, even though the law contains the terms mentioned in § 2.[125]

If the ignorance alleged is "crass or supine" it has no effect on *latae sententiae* penalties.

---

123 John J. McGrath, Comparative Study on Crime and its Imputability Ecclesiastical in Criminal Law and in American Criminal Law 47 (1957).
124 Code of Canon Law, Canon 2229 §1 (1917).
125 Code of Canon Law, Canon 2229 §1 (1917).

B. Drunkenness

Second, drunkenness, omission of due diligence and weakness of mind or the overwhelming effect of passion diminishes, though do not excuse one from responsibility for *latae sententiae* penalty. The Code at 2229 §2 consists of:

Canon 2229 - §2, 2° Ebrietas, omissio debitae diligentiea, mentis debilitas, impetus passionis, si, non obstante imputabilitatis deminutione, actio sit adhuc graviter culpabilis, a poenis latae sententiae non excusant.[126]	Drunkenness, omission of due care, mental weakness, and heat of passion do not excuse from penalties *latae sententiae*, if notwithstanding the diminution of the liability the action was gravely sinful.[127]

C. Fear and Necessity

Third, grave fear/necessity can be a viable defense challenge. The 1917 Code limited the defense of fear to those circumstances not dealing with a contempt for the faith or of ecclesiastical authority. The Code makes plain this restriction.

Canon 2229 - §3, 3° Metus gravis, si delictum vergat in contemptum fidei aut ecclesiasticae auctoritatis vel in publicum animarum damnum, a poenis latae sententiae nullatenus eximit.[128]	Canon 2229 - §3, 3° Grave fear does not exempt from penalties *latae sententiae*, if the offense entails contempt of the faith or of ecclesiastical authority, or public injury or souls.[129]

Actions which are deleterious to the salvation of souls, *"publicum animarum damnum"* disallowed the defense of *grave fear* under the 1917 Code.

---

126 Code of Canon Law, Canon 2229 §3, 2° (1917).
127 Stanislaus Woywod, A Practical Commentary on the Code of Canon Law 466 (1952).
128 Code of Canon Law, Canon 2229 §3, 3° (1917).
129 Stanislaus Woywod, A Practical Commentary on the Code of Canon Law 466-467 (1952).

This exception to a rule of extenuating circumstances exists even despite the Code's recognition that "fear/necessity and hardship can diminish imputability under Canon 2205, except in similar situations involving contempt of authority or damage to the faithful.

Canon 2205 - §3. Si vero actus sit intrinsece malus aut vergat in contemptum fidei vel ecclesiasticae auctoritatis vel in animarum damnum, causae, de quibus in §2, delicti imputabilitatem minuunt quidem, sed non auferunt.[130]

Canon 2205 - §3. If, however, an act is intrinsically evil and involves itself in a contempt of the faith or of ecclesiastical authority or works toward the ruination of souls, excuses, based upon §2, diminish the imputability of the delict but do not eliminate it.

The 1917 Code classifies unauthorized consecration as damaging to the faithful. It could be posed that the Archbishop was in error because of his "duty to prevent harm by carefully foreseeing (or knowing) the results of an action; and, the duty to prevent, as far as this is possible and obligatory, a foreseen (or known) injury from going into effect."[131]

Canonist John McGrath highlights this stern and unyielding restriction when the offense deals with the salvation of souls:

Finally, some crimes will draw people away from the faith or from a sound moral life, and result in their eternal damnation. These crimes endanger another's salvation either because of the scandal involved, or by the very nature of the act. No man can be excused of a crime because of fear, necessity or hardship if the salvation of another's soul is the price. Among such delicts should be included: the administration of the sacraments to those who are forbidden to receive

---

130 Code of Canon Law, Canon 2205, §3 (1917).
131 Robert Swoboda, Ignorance in Relation to the Imputability of Delicts, Innocent 108 (1941).

them, the absolution of one's accomplice, the consecration of a bishop without a papal mandate, simony
in regard to the sacraments, the discarding of the
clerical garb and the violation of the obligation of
celibacy when scandal would be involved.[132]

Regrettably for the Archbishop, the grave fear/necessity
defense would not be favorably received if the 1917 Code
was the authority relied upon. Among the deficits listed
above is *"the consecration of a bishop without papal mandate"*.
Canonist Alan McCoy, O.F.M. characterizes any action of
contempt of the Faith or ecclesiastical authority by noting the
supremacy of the act itself over the necessary mental state.

> First, it must be stressed that the contempt of the
> faith or of authority mentioned here must not be
> understood as subjective contempt formally present
> in the intention of the agent. It is rather the objective
> contempt resulting from the very nature of the act, or
> at least from the concrete circumstances in which the
> act is placed. The legislator indicates this by speak-
> ing of the act which tends to such contempt, and not
> of the contempt of the agent.[133]

While not all acts of disobedience result in a finding of
contempt, it is a rational conclusion that a *latae sententiae*
violation, of which there are only *seven*, would qualify.
McCoy tries to set up the requirements:

> Clearly then, the concept of this contempt must
> be restricted so as to include only those delicts which
> involve contempt of the faith or of authority in a

132 John J. McGrath, Comparative Study on Crime and its Imputability
    Ecclesiastical in Criminal Law and in American Criminal Law 68-69 (1957).
133 Alan Edward McCoy, Force and Fear in Relation to Delictual Imputability
    and Penal Responsibility, An Historical Synopsis and Commentary 92 (1944).

special manner. This will be the case either because they are of their very nature directly aimed against the truths of faith or against persons constituted in authority, or because they violate a precept in such a way that by reason of circumstances such contempt necessarily and directly redounds to faith or to authority.[134]

Other exempting circumstances under the 1917 Code include the following, though notably are not germane to the defense of the Archbishop.

    1. *Debilitas mentis.* (C. 2201, §4). (Mental illness or insanity.)
    2. *Minor aetas* (c. 2204). (Infancy.)
    3. *Legitimae tutelae contra iniustum agressorum, si debitum servetur moderamen, sicut etiam causa provocationis* (c. 2205, §4). (Self-defense.)
    4. *Passio, in quantum deliberationem mentis et consensum voluntatis menuit* (c. 2206). (Passion.)[135]

Further discussion on the fear/necessity and hardship defense will be found in Chapters 8.

III. Extenuating Circumstances Under the 1983 Code

Most practical and scholarly accounts indicate an extreme liberalization of the role extenuating circumstances play in a judgment of imputability. Canonist Count Neri Capponi when asked to compare the 1917 and the 1983 Code's treatment of such circumstances remarked:

---

134 Alan Edward McCoy, *Force and Fear in Relation to Delictual Imputability and Penal Responsibility,* An Historical Synopsis and Commentary 93 (1944).
135 Code of Canon Law, Canons 2201 §§3-4, 2202 - 2206 (1917).

But I would also argue that the excommunication *may* not in fact be valid, because the allowances for extenuating circumstances in the 1983 Code are such that Archbishop Lefebvre would have easily gotten away without being excommunicated. He could have argued state of necessity, he could have argued a host of extenuating circumstances.

You can't have your cake and eat it, too. Rome wanted a lenient code, they filled the code with extenuating circumstances so that practically no penalty applies, but they have to pay the consequences. They can't go back to the 1917 Code to punish Lefebvre when he committed his crime after 1983.[136]

His caricature of the 1983 Code is less than charitable:

It's a joke. But then if you've chosen to establish a joke, you have to go by it. You can't say because it's a joke, I'm going back to what doesn't exist anymore.[137]

Joke or not, the 1983 *Code of Canon Law* is the rule applicable in our current analysis. Jose Bernacer reflects on the new spirit in weighing extenuating circumstances.

In this title, the legislator shows a lot of understanding towards the delinquent. Included in this title are many subjective circumstances that may affect the responsibility of the subject and so *exempt* him

---

136 Note, *Church Law, Jargon-Free and Interview with Count Neri Capponi*, 2 Latin Mass Magazine 14, 16 (May-June 1993).
137 Note, *Church Law, Jargon-Free and Interview with Count Neri Capponi*, 2 Latin Mass Magazine 14, 16 (May-June 1993).

from the penalty or the legislator should *temper* the penalty or *substitute* it with a penance.[138]

Ladislas Orsy calls the 1983 canonical approach a beckoning to be an inquiring mind, a means to new "horizons." That those who fail to accept "change" are unable "to move from one horizon into another."[139] As a symbol of our incapacity to grasp the new "horizon," he cited Marcel Lefebvre:

A most recent example: Archbishop Lefebvre could not bring himself to enter into the horizon of Vatican Council II. No amount of conceptual explanation (undoubtedly given by many) could bring him around; only a radical conversion could have disposed him to accept the Council.[140]

The bizarre irony of Orsy's condemnation of Lefebvre leaps out when assessing his interpretation of Canon Law:

We are a social body growing in understanding. The point is in the movement. If the whole group, and every member of it, is growing, there cannot be any other correct interpretation, even of seemingly rigid laws, than the one which takes the evolutionary process into account.[141]

Understanding, a *rejection of rigidity* in law, and a fluidity of legal concepts are not applied in the case of the Archbishop. These principles find no solace in historical tradi-

---

138 Jose L. Bernacer, Sanctions in the Church Readings, Cases, Materials in Canon Law, 422, 426 (1990).
139 Ladislas Orsy, Theology and Canon Law: New Horizons for Legislation and Interpretation 15 (1992).
140 Ladislas Orsy, Theology and Canon Law: New Horizons for Legislation and Interpretation 34 (1992).
141 Ladislas Orsy, Theology and Canon Law: New Horizons for Legislation and Interpretation 63 (1992).

tion, but only rest in the magic of Vatican II. It is patently absurd to claim the "new spirit" of canonical norms apply to all but those who exhibit conservative tendencies.

Against this inexplicable backdrop, the Code does, without reservation, liberalize, extend and expand the array of extenuating circumstances that exempt or excuse or minimize imputability.

A. Exemption and Excuse Under the 1983 Code

At Canon 1323, an action is *not* subject to penalties even though an external violation has taken place. The provision encompasses seven extenuating circumstances:

Canon 1323 - Nulli poenae est obnoxius qui, cum legem vel praeceptum violavit:

1° sextum decimum aetatis annum nondum explevit;

2° sine culpa ignoravit se legem vel praeceptum violare; ignorantiae autem inadvertentia et error aequiparantur;

3° egit ex vi physica vel ex casu fortuito quem praevidere vel cui praeviso occurrere non potuit;

4° metu gravi, quamvis relative tantum, coactus egit, aut ex necessitate vel gravi incommodo, nisi tamen actus sit intrinsece malus aut vergat in animarum damnum;

5° legitimae tutelae causa contra iniustum sui vel alterius aggressorem egit, debitum servans moderamen;

Canon 1323 - The following are not subject to penalties when they have violated a law or precept:

1° a person who has not yet completed the sixteen years of age;

2° a person who without any fault was unaware of violating a law or precept; however, inadvertence and error are equivalent to ignorance;

3° a person who acted out of physical force or in virtue of a mere accident which could neither be foreseen nor prevented when foreseen;

4° a person who acted out of grave fear, even if only relatively grave, or out of necessity or out of serious inconvenience unless the act is intrinsically evil or verges on harm to souls;

5° a person who for the sake of legitimate self-defense or defense of another acted against an unjust aggressor with due moderation;

6° rationis usu carebat, firmis praescriptis cann. 1324, §1, n. 2 et 1325;	6° a person who lacked the use of reason with due regard for the prescriptions of Canon 1324 §1, n.2 and 1325;
7° sine culpa putavit aliquam adesse ex circumstantiis, de quibus in nn. 4 vel 5.[142]	7° a person who without any fault felt that the circumstances in nn. 4 or 5 were verified.[143]

In modern ecclesiastical jurisprudence, actions are tempered by mitigating forces. McDonough remarks cogently:

> Yet, they are consistent with the understanding of imputability as resulting from a deliberate and free human act, and with recognition that lack of either deliberation or freedom as well as various degrees of impaired deliberation or freedom have direct consequences for imputability and penal liability.[144]

Of particular interest above are points *four* and *seven*. In the former, an actor who can demonstrate that his actions arise from grave fear, even slight fear, or resulted from necessity, can be excused. At §7, a person who lacks malicious intent or "fault" because be believes the circumstances cited in §4 or §5 to be true is also exempted. Oratorian canonist T.C.G. Glover argues that §7 metes out no punishment unless the action possessed grave moral imputability (fault). He comments:

> This means, in the moral theologian's terminology, subjective mortal sin. The Archbishop has made it clear many times that his primary purpose in consecrating successors is to ensure a future supply of traditional priests to provide the laity with Mass and the sacraments. He acted only after years of thought,

---

142 Code of Canon Law, Canon 1323 (1983).
143 Code of Canon Law, Canon 1323 (1983).
144 Elizabeth McDonough, *A Novus Habitus Mentis for Sanctions in the Church*, 48 The Jurist 727, 735 (1988).

and many months of protracted negotiations with the
Holy See; and a similar intention and careful consideration can be discerned in the other five bishops.
Even if the final decision is judged a mistake, it cannot
amount to subjective mortal sin.[145]

The modern Code is thoroughly silent on what acts
"verge on harm to souls" — the only qualifying language
being at §4. Under the 1917 Code, action that constitutes
"publicum animarium damnum" was listed and qualified — the
illegal or unwarranted consecration of a bishop being
amongst those listed. The 1983 Code language "verges" is a
far cry from the absolute pronouncements in the former
Code. Coriden, Green and Heintschel claim that acts prompt-
ing "pastoral damages"[146] will never be thoroughly excusable.
The policy behind this principle is:

> This seems to be true because certain higher val-
> ues are at stake which the legislator cannot neglect.[147]

Thus, one could advocate that the actions of the Archbishop could not be excused by grave fear or necessity on
account of the exceptional language "the act. . . verges on a
harm to souls." When compared to the 1917 Code's qualifier,
*"contemptum fidei vel ecclesiasticae auctoritatis, aut in animarum
damnum"*[148] the 1983 proviso is, at best, nebulous. The language of the 1983 as well as the 1917 Code is to be interpreted
according to its plain meaning. Ecclesiastical law looks to

---

145 Glover, *Schism and Archbishop Lefebvre* in Is Tradition Excommunicated?
     Where is Catholicism Today? 97, 98 (Society of Saint Pius X, ed., 1993).
146 James A. Coriden, Thomas J. Green, & Donald E. Heintschel, The Code of
     Canon Law, A Text and Commentary 902 (1990).
147 James A. Coriden, Thomas J. Green, & Donald E. Heintschel, The Code of
     Canon Law, A Text and Commentary 902 (1990).
148 Code of Canon Law, Canon 2205 (1917).

what is written, what is commonly understood, what is uniformly agreed upon. The 1917 Code sets out interpretative parameters:

Leges ecclesiasticae intelligendae sunt secundum propriam verborum significationem in textu et contextu consideratum: quae si dubia et obscura manserit, ad locos Codicis parallelos, si qui sint, ad legis finem ac circumstantias et ad mentem legislatoris est recurrendum.[149]	The ecclesiastical laws are to be interpreted according to the proper meaning of the terms of the law considered in their context. If the meaning of the terms remain doubtful or obscure, one must have recourse to parallel passages of the Code (if there are any), or to the purpose of the law and its circumstances, and the intention of the legislator.[150]

Canonist Ludovicus Bender's dissertation on the interpretation of ecclesiastical law, appreciates the rule of plain meaning:

Huic legi applicatur operatio intellectualis. Obiectum seu lex est semper aliquod datum obiective existens.[151]	The operation of the intellect is applied to this or that law. For the objective or end of law is always that given by objective existence or reality.

Moreover, law does not depend on emotion or whim to interpret content when it is only known by its objective existence. What it says is basically what it is!

The 1983 Code upholds this view at Canon 17.

---

149 Code of Canon Law, Canon 18 (1917).
150 Stanislaus Woywod, A Practical Commentary on the Code of Canon Law 13 (1952).
151 Ludovicus Bender, Legum Ecclesiasticarum Interpretatio et Suppletio 109 (1961).

Canon 17 - Leges ecclesiasticae intellegendae sunt secundum propriam verborum significationem in textu et contentu consideratam; quae si dubia et obscura manserit, ad locos parallelos, si qui sint, ad legis finem ac circumstantias et ad mentem legislatoris est recurrendum.[152]

Can. 17 - Ecclesiastical laws are to be understood in accord with the proper meaning of the words considered in their text and context. If the meaning remains doubtful and obscure, recourse is to be taken to parallel passages, if such exist, to the purpose and the circumstances of the law, and to the mind of the legislator.[153]

Further enhancing this position is Canon 18 mandating *strict* interpretation of the law when the application of penalties is involved:

Canon 18 - Leges quae poenam statuunt aut liberum iurium exercitium coarctant aut exceptionem a lege continent, strictae subsunt interpretationi.[154]

Canon 18 - Laws which establish a penalty or restrict the free exercise of rights or which contain an exception to the law are subject to a strict interpretation.[155]

With these policies in mind, the 1983 Code's less than descriptive "verges on harms to soul" is a matter of discretionary interpretation. The Code of 1917, at least imprecisely, enunciated some standards that dislodge the defense of grave fear and necessity. We can infer, to some extent, what action is morally wrong, and therefore inexcusable, because it is intrinsically evil. When the 1917 Code directly lists conduct that is in "contempt of ecclesiastical authority" some objective measure is afforded. Admittedly, *"publicum amimarum damnum"* is an unquantifiable standard.

When compared, the 1983 Code eliminates ecclesiastical contempt — an omission integral to the defense of Marcel Lefebvre. All that remains is the term, "verges." This being so, is it a plausible contention that Marcel Lefebvre's actions

---

152 Code of Canon Law, Canon 17 (1983).
153 Code of Canon Law, Canon 17 (1983).
154 Code of Canon Law, Canon 18 (1983).
155 Code of Canon Law, Canon 18 (1983).

are triggered by his desire to ruin souls? Is his motivation to destroy the Church institution and limit the salvation of the masses? Canonist Von Rudolf Kaschewsky attempts to gauge the intent and heart of Marcel Lefebvre in the matter of the ordination.

5. Es steht fest und wird auch wohl kaum ernsthaft bestritten, daß durch den nachkonziliaren Kurs insbesondere in der Priesterausbildung eine akute Gefährdung geistlicher Güter", nämlich des Glaubens, der Moral, del Gottesdienstes innerhalb der Kirche zu verzeichnen ist. Zum Nachweis dieser Behauptung braucht hier nur auf einen Vielzahl von Beiträgen, auch und gerade in unserer Zeitschift, verwiesen zu werden.[156]

5. The question is, can the endangerment of spiritual matters be countered? Nobody will contradict that a good way is to train and shape good priests. But to the questions on how, when and where and what else can be done to keep them from the bad influences of the world, the answer is: Nothing.[157]

Any cursory understanding of the life and times of the Archbishop could never lead to the conclusion he relishes ruination of souls. A Catholic prelate who attended and supported the Archbishop at the Ecône ordinations and who also incurred the penalty of excommunication by his alleged complicity, Bishop Antonio de Castro Mayer, paints a miserable picture of the strains and stresses in the modern Church, and the reaction of Marcel Lefebvre to its state:

This is the situation in which we find ourselves. We live in an unprecedented crisis in the Church, a crisis which touches it in its essence, in its substance even, which is the Holy Sacrifice of the Mass and the Catholic priesthood, the two mysteries essentially united, because without the holy priesthood there is

---

156 Von Rudolf Kaschewsky, *Zur Frage der Bischofsweihe ohne Päpstlichen Auftrag,* Vra Voce Korrespontenz 86, 87 (sum. 1988).
157 Von Rudolf Kaschewsky, *Zur Frage der Bischofsweihe ohne Päpstlichen Auftrag,* Vra Voce Korrespontenz 86, 87 (sum. 1988).

no Holy Sacrifice of the Mass, and by consequence, no form of public worship whatsoever. Equally, it is on this basis that one constructs the social reign of Our Lord Jesus Christ.

Because of this, since the conservation of the priesthood and of the Holy Mass is at stake, and in spite of the requests and the pressure brought to bear by many, I am here to accomplish my duty; to make a public profession of Faith.[158]

Accepting the indiscernible standard "*verges*" in the 1983 Code, especially when compared rigidly to the 1917 Code (*contemptum fidei vel ecclesiastical auctoritas*), it is sensible to conclude that the act of consecration could be excused by fear, either grave or simple, or by necessity under the 1983 Code. The analysis of said defense will be covered thoroughly in Chapter 8.

1983 Canon 1323 emphasizes the removal of or complete dissipation of imputability. To successfully overcome evidentiary standards delineated at §1-7, the advocate must disclose:

. . .such persons are still not subject to a penalty since there is a significant diminishing of their freedom or awareness of the implications of their activity: hence there is no real imputability.[159]

B. Mitigation and Dimunition Under the 1983 Code

One other tactic in defense strategy is feasible: not the assertion that imputability should be excused, but a claim

158 Antonio de Castro Mayer, *Declaration* in Is Tradition Excommunicated? Where is Catholicism Today?, 95 (Society of Saint Pius X., ed., 1993).
159 James A. Coriden, Thomas J. Green, & Donald E. Heintschel, The Code of Canon Law, A Text and Commentary 902 (1990).

that imputability, even though it remains, changes form — either minimized or mitigated. Canon 1324 enunciates circumstances or conditions that will moderate final judgement or suggest a penal alternative:

Canon 1324 - §1. Violationis auctor non eximitur a poena, sed poena lege vel praecepto statuta temperari debet vel in eius locum paenitentia adhiberi, si delictum patratum sit:

1° ab eo, qui rationis usum imperfectum tantum habuerit;

2° ab eo qui rationis usu carebat propter ebrietatem aliamve similem mentis perturbationem, quae culpabilis fuerit;

3° ex gravi passionis aestu, qui non omnem tamen mentis deliberationem et voluntatis consensum praecesserit et impedierit, et dummodo passio ipsa ne fuerit voluntarie excitata vel nutrita;

4° a minore, qui aetatem sedecim annorum explevit;

5° ab eo, qui metu gravi, quamvis relative tantum, coactus est, aut ex necessitate vel gravi incommodo, si delictum sit intrinsece malum vel in animarum damnum vergat;

6° ab eo, qui legitimae tutelae causa contra iniustum sui vel alterius aggressorem egit, nec tamen debitum servavit moderamen;

7° adversus aliquem graviter et iniuste provocantem;

8° ab eo, qui per errorem, ex sua tamen culpa, putavit aliquam adesse ex circumstantiis, de quibus in can. 1323, nn. 4 vel 5;

9° ab eo, qui sine culpa ignoravit poenam legi vel praecepto esse adnexam;

Canon 1324 - §1. One who violates a law or precept is not exempt from a penalty but the penalty set by law or precept must be tempered or a penance substituted in its place if the offense was committed:

1° by a person with only the imperfect use of reason;

2° by a person who lacked the use of reason due to drunkenness or another similar mental disturbance which was culpable;

3° in the serious heat of passion which did not precede and impede all deliberation of mind and consent of will as long as the passion itself had not been voluntarily stirred up or fostered;

4° by a minor who has completed the age of sixteen years;

5° by a person who was forced through grave fear, even if only relatively grave, or through necessity or serious inconvenience, if the offense was intrinsically evil or verged on harm to souls.

6° by a person who for the sake of legitimate self-defense or defense of another acted against an unjust aggressor but without due moderation;

7° against one gravely and unjustly provoking it;

8° by one who erroneously yet culpably thought one of the circumstances in Canon 1323, nn 4 and 5 was verified;

9° by one who without any fault was unaware that a penalty was attached to the law or precept;

10° ab eo, qui egit sine plena imputabilitate, dummodo haec gravis permanserit.[160]	10° by one who acted without full imputability provided there was grave imputability.[161]

Relevant to this analysis is §4, §8 and §10. As to the matter of fear and necessity, the modern Code is far more generous than its 1917 counterpart. Fear can be grave *(metu gravi)* and even relatively slight *(quamvis relative tantum).* Joined with necessity is the standard "serious inconvenience *(gravi incommodo).* Even *when* the action "verges on harm to soul" *(animarum damnum vergat),* the Code allows mitigation. Thus, the worst case for the Archbishop is the rejection of a complete defense to full imputability under 1323 §4, though a finding that his conduct *(animarum damnnum vergat)* harmed souls would *still* allow a diminution of imputability. After an examination of the *latae sententiae* penalty imposed, it would appear Church authorities gave little credence to Canon 1324 §5. Then again, those who made the determination are not convinced that arguments of fear and necessity have any bearing whatsoever.

At best, this type of judgment is premature. The canonical question was, and still is a procedural one: Can the Archbishop raise the defense of fear and necessity, despite any harm to souls by this action, to extenuate his *latae sententiae* penalty? The answer is unreservedly affirmative.

At §8 of Canon 1324, the actor is permitted to assert defenses if he believes that his fear, his notion of necessitous circumstances, or action and self-defense was true *subjectively,* but even wrong *objectively.* Posed another way, the actor knows his action is wrong but he believes in its justification. Coriden, Green and Heintschel comment:

---

160   Code of Canon Law, Canon 1324 §1 (1983).
161   Code of Canon Law, Canon 1324 §1 (1983).

Also subject to a lesser penalty is the person who erroneously but culpably thinks that the excusing causes of grave fear or legitimate self-defense were verified in a given situation (8°).

This is actually similar to the factor of culpable ignorance of the penalty mentioned earlier.[162]

By incorporating the provisions of Canon 1323 §4 and §5 into the heart of Canon 1324, the 1983 Code has dramatically altered the provisions of 1917. Not only can the actor assert he has *no* imputability because of fear and necessity, absent a holding that the action "verges", a seemingly impossible burden, but also, even if his action to remove imputability bears no fruit, an identical claim to diminish imputability can be proffered.

Referencing Canon 1323 §4 and §5 into 1324 makes this *latae sententiae* penalty even less likely. Coriden, Green and Heintschel see the discretionary ambiance of the 1983 provision,

> The Canon provides ample latitude for judicial or administrative discretion in dealing with an offender, and it reflects an awareness of the difficulty in providing an exhaustive catalogue of factors that diminish imputability (§2).[163]

At §10, the Archbishop can argue confidently that his actions were effected by fear, necessity and the belief that his action of consecration was crucial to the survival of his order. Intelligent defense strategists would charge that these influences make *full* imputability an impossibility. Considering

162 James A. Coriden, Thomas J. Green, & Donald E. Heintschel, The Code of Canon Law, A Text and Commentary 903-04 (1990).
163 James A. Coriden, Thomas J. Green, & Donald E. Heintschel, The Code of Canon Law, A Text and Commentary 903 (1990).

the history of the Archbishop, various factors would impede any formal judgment as to his full and unequivocal imputability. Coriden, Green and Heintschel further charge:

> Furthermore, in light of the traditional principle that penalties are proportionate to grave imputability, the law states generically that if there were no full imputability, for whatever reason, but at least grave imputability, a diminished penalty is warranted (10°).[164]

So, in the most extreme scenario, the Archbishop must receive a benefit of mitigation as the Code's commentary points out:

> b) The violator of the law is not exempt from all penalty but the penalty laid down in the law or in the administrative order *must be mitigated*, or a penance must be substituted, if the offense was accomplished by someone believing through an error, even if culpable, that he was in a circumstance foreseen in Canon 1323, n. 4 and 5.[165]

Canon 1324 at §2 admonishes ecclesiastical jurists, to lessen the seriousness of offenses when these types of circumstances exist.

§2. Idem potest iudex facere, si qua alia adsit circumstantia, quae delicti gravitatem deminuat.[166]

§2. A judge can act in the same manner if any other circumstance exists which would lessen the seriousness of the offense.[167]

---

164 James A. Coriden, Thomas J. Green, & Donald E. Heintschel, The Code of Canon Law, A Text and Commentary 904 (1990).
165 Code of Canon Law, Canon 1324, n.18 (1983).
166 Code of Canon Law, Canon 1324 §2 (1983).
167 Code of Canon Law, Canon 1324 §2 (1983).

Finally, §3 of the Canon affirmatively negates the legality and procedural regularity of any *latae sententiae* penalty when mitigating circumstances exist. Coriden, Green and Heintschel see §3 as probative on the matter of Code liberalization and its hesitancy to impose penalties:

> This is another example of legislative caution relative to such penalties. It embodies a concern that normally there should be some kind of official intervention to weigh the penal significance of the factors mentioned in paragraph one.[168]

By any salient standard, the action of the Archbishop and the penalties imposed are lacking in canonical foundation.

LEGAL HOLDING 2.1: Therefore, given the express restriction of contempt of ecclesiastical authority cases under Canon 2229 §3, and Canon 2205 as a means of excuse, exemption or mitigation of the act of consecration makes the Archbishop imputable under the 1917 Code of Canon Law.

LEGAL HOLDING 2.2: Any contempt of ecclesiastical authority denies the defense of grave fear or necessity making the Archbishop imputable under the 1917 Code, at Canon 2229 §3.

LEGAL HOLDING 2.3: Grave fear and necessity could remove imputability if the action of the Archbishop did not *"animarum damnum vergat"* under the 1983 Code, at Canon 1323, 4°.

---

168 James A. Coriden, Thomas J. Green, & Donald E. Heintschel, The Code of Canon Law, A Text and Commentary 904 (1990).

LEGAL HOLDING 2.4: That the Archbishop's demonstration of fear, either grave or slight, could mitigate and diminish his imputability according to Canon 1324, 4° (1983).

LEGAL HOLDING 2.5: That the Archbishop's demonstration that his belief, as to fear and necessity of action, was held in good faith, even if erroneously, is a basis for diminished imputability under Canon 1323, 4° and 5°.

LEGAL HOLDING 2.6: That the Archbishop's proof of mitigating factors, such as fear, grave hardship, necessity, as an impetus to the consecration, will result in diminished imputability as provided in Canon 1324 at 2°, 4°, 5°, 8°, 10°, and 12°.

LEGAL HOLDING 2.7: That the Archbishop's demonstration of any of Canon 1324's factors diminishing responsibility, will mitigate a *latae sententiae* penalty under Canon 1324 at 2°, 4°, 5°, 8°, and 10°.

The canonical inquiry now turns to a more esoteric discussion of specific defenses.

CHAPTER 7

Fear and Imputability

LEGAL ISSUE #3: Whether the Archbishop's act of consecration, without papal mandate, can be excused on account of fear, or in the alternative, be a means to diminish imputability.

I. Fear: Exemption and Excuse

For all practical purposes, as noted earlier, *fear*, under the Code of 1917, was a permissible defense tactic in all cases except *"contemptum fidei aut ecclesiasticae auctoritatis"* or where the action is *"animarum damnum vergat."*[168] The precision of Canon 2229 §3 undercuts viable canonical defense arguments on behalf of the Archbishop. Consecrating bishops, without papal mandate, despite internal justifications, is an action listed as contemptuous to authority and damaging to souls. Whether one agrees with the Canon's equity is irrelevant. Under the 1917 Code, fear was a losing rationale.

Hence, grave fear or slight fear could not successfully be employed in the defense of the Archbishop under the terms and conditions of the 1917 Code. However, how fear is

___
168 Code of Canon Law, Canon 2229 §3 (1917).

defined, how it is applied to cases and interpreted relies upon historical precedent and definitional inquiry since the modern Code is largely silent.

Fear is an irascible passion that has the capacity to overwhelm, by its appetency, the rational faculty. It is when fear dominates good judgment and reason that fear can serve as either excuse or mitigating factor. When deliberation and freedom of will are infected by fear, imputability is removed.[169]

In the Code of 1983, Canon 1323 §4 excuses, removes imputability, when the actor's conduct results from *metu gravi*, and even *gravis relative tantum*, relatively slight fear. Bear in mind, that this defense principle is conditionally applicable, depending on how the jurist interprets "verges on harm to souls" (See previous discussion at Chapter 6). Fear *(metus)* is a compulsive force. "It is a confusion."[170] Fear modifies the will. As canonist McCoy portrays it:

> It is called a confusion or perturbation of the mind *(mentis trepidatio)* to indicate that it is an affection of the mind or will *(affectio animi)*.[171]

Fear arises from internal causes *(ab intrinseco)* or from external sources, like the threat of another soldier in battle. There are varying degrees of fear from relatively grave, *(metus vanus)* to slight or absolutely grave fear. Resolving whether or not the Archbishop was moved by fear in any form is both an objective and subjective judgment. How do

169 Alan E. McCoy, Force and Fear in Relation to Delictual Imputability and Penal Responsibility 77 (1944).
170 Alan E. McCoy, Force and Fear in Relation to Delictual Imputability and Penal Responsibility 78 (1944).
171 Alan E. McCoy, Force and Fear in Relation to Delictual Imputability and Penal Responsibility 78 (1944).

we know fear at all? What makes people afraid in the first place? How could one fear for the current state of the Catholic Church?

Evaluate the content of an interview with Bishop Castro de Mayer — tagged an "accomplice" at Ecône:

L'excommunication vous laisse-t-elle indifférent?

Indifférent, non. Même invalide elle m'attriste, parce qu'elle montre le lamentable état où se trouve la partie humaine de l'Église. Elle montre l'intensité de l'aversion que les membres actuels de la Hiérarchie nourrissent envers ce que l'Élise a toujours fait. Alors qu'ils demandent pardon aux pires ennemis de l'Élise, les luthériens, les anglicans, les juifs, ils éloignent de leur communion les fils les plus fidèles de la Saints Église.

Quel message voulez-vous adresser à nos lecteurs?

Demeurez fermes dans la Foi! Gardez soigneusement le trésor qui vous a été confié, la Tradition catholique! Par la grâce de Dieu, je vous ai transmis cela même que j'ai reçu de l'Élise, ce que j'ai appris au Séminaire à Rome: la doctrine des Pères de L'Élise, des Apôtres, de Notre-Seigneur: "Tradidi quod et accepi"! Qu'est-ce que je peux désirer sinon que tous les catholiques gardent inviolable ce trésor inestimable?[172]

Are you indifferent to the excommunication?

Indifferent, no. Though invalid, it saddens me, because it shows the lamentable state in which the human part of the Church finds itself. It shows the intensity of the aversion the actual members of the hierarchy feel against what the Church has always done. When they ask forgiveness of the worst enemies of the Church, the Lutherans, the Anglicans, the Jews, they remove from their communion the truest sons of the Holy Church!

What message would you like to address to our readers?

Remain firm in the Faith! Guard carefully the treasure you have been given: The Catholic Tradition! By the grace of God, I have transmitted to you the same I have received from the Church, what I have learned at the Seminary in Rome! The doctrine of the Fathers of the Church, the Apostles, of Our Lord. "Tradidi quod et accepi"! What else can I wish for, but that all Catholics keep this inestimable treasure inviolable?[173]

---

172 Entretien Accordé par S.E. Monseigneur Antonio De Castro Mayer, Évêque Émérite De Campos (Brésil), À Un Journal Local (Sept. 29, 1983).
173 Entretien Accordé par S.E. Monseigneur Antonio De Castro Mayer, Évêque Émérite De Campos (Brésil), À Un Journal Local (Sept. 29, 1983).

Fear is an urgency that can only be ameliorated by a response to the criminal evil it presents. The notion of fear cannot be universally applied, except that fear does not ensue from trifles. Fear is not insanity but rational resistance to perceived evil.

II. Fear and the Archbishop

In the eyes of Marcel Lefebvre, the modern church and its governance signified a trek into theological and magisterial oblivion. His mind evidences a fear about the status quo and his resistance represents a lashing out, a verbal barrage against the onslaught of a tangible evil. In this sense, fear is not a sign of weakness but a recognition of error. The Archbishop viewed his role as a bastion, a bulwark, in a last thin blue line between barbarism and the Christian community. His concerns are multifaceted:

> 1) religious liberty, implying a discussion of the whole question of the legitimacy and/or desirability of religious pluralism within the structure of non-confessional states. . . ;
> 2) ecumenism, implying a discussion of the nature and extent of the Catholic claim that it is the one *true* Church of Jesus Christ; and
> 3) humanism, implying a discussion of the manner and extent to which human life and human progress can be the final aim of human striving, of the extent to which the divine, the sacred, the transcendent are linked to, coherent with, or disconnected from the human, the profane, the everyday.[174]

---

174 Robert Moynihan, *The Curia's Dilemma*, Inside the Vatican 8, 12 (Aug./Sept. 1993).

THE CASE OF
ARCHBISHOP
MARCEL
LEFEBVRE

TRIAL BY
CANON LAW

A PICTORIAL OF
THE CONSECRATIONS

Arrival of Bishop Antonio de Cast

Iayer at Ecône, 25 June, 1988

rchbishop Lefebvre waits
r the arrival of Bishop
ntonio de Castro Mayer
˝ the diocese of Campos,
razil, who will co-
nsecrate with him four
w bishops.

The two bishops greet
each other outside the
seminary at Ecône, in
Switzerland, equally
convinced of the
necessity of the
consecrations.

Bishop de Castro Mayer puts
incense in the thurible while
Archbishop Lefebvre looks on.
Of very nearly the same age as the
Archbishop, he was here being
received solemnly as a Bishop at
the Seminary of Ecône on June
25, in preparation for the
ceremony of June 30th. He had
made the long and gruelling
journey from Brazil even though
in frail health.

Ordination Ceremony

On June 29, Feast of Saints Peter and Paul, eve of the episcopal consecrations, there took place at Ecône the customary ceremony of priestly ordinations. The number of traditional Catholic priests standing at the altar just after laying hands on the 16 new priests (kneeling) was larger in 1988 than it had ever been to date.

After the June 29 ordinations, the newly ordained priests together with Archbishop Lefebvre and Bishop de Castro Mayer stand in the courtyard at Ecône.

The Consecrations, 30 June, 1988

The four new bishops-to-be process down the aisle of a cathedral-tent erected on the lawn of the Ecône seminary for the occasion. Estimates placed the crowd which wrapped all three sides of the sanctuary at 16,000. Some 150 seminarians and at least 200 priests from all over the world were in attendance.

The Professions of Faith of the Tw

"

We are not schismatic and we do not want to found a new Church. Our attachment to the eternal Church is obvious. But today there is an emergency situation. The 'modern' Church is apostatizing; it is not doing what it was founded to do. What the Church has always condemned is now permitted: liberalism and communism are acceptable; ecumenism is in the process of destroying our Faith. If I too were to teach error, I would aid in this destruction and the loss of souls.

"

(Archbishop Lefebvre explains his decision to proceed with the consecrations)

shops

"

When our Faith is in danger, then
we are bound to publicly manifest it,
and today this is the case.
This crisis touches the Church and
her very essence: the Holy Sacrifice
of the Mass. For there is no Sacrifice
without priests, and no priests
without bishops, and everything is
built upon this Holy Sacrifice.
Therefore I am here to fulfill my
duty and openly profess my Faith.

"

*(Bishop de Castro Mayer's
Profession at the Consecrations)*

The ceremony proceeds. First, twenty questions are posed to the bishops-elect about their willingness to fulfill their duties and advance in virtue. Then, the four priests in chasubles prostrate themselves before the main altar while the *Litany of the Saints* is sung to obtain the intercession of all the saints in heaven. Within a few minutes will come the imposition of hands by Archbishop Lefebvre and Bishop de Castro Mayer which actually makes the priests into bishops. Afterwards ensues the consecrations of their heads, hands, and rings, the concelebration of Holy Mass, the imposition of the mitre, crozier, and gloves and their enthronement, the *Te Deum* of triumph and thanksgiving, the first blessing of the bishop, and the solemn recessional of all the clergy.

Born at Sierre (Valais), Switzerland, **_Fr. Bernard Fellay_** (below) entered the seminary of Ecône in 1977. He was ordained to the priesthood on June 29, 1982, by Archbishop Lefebvre. Immediately afterwards he was nominated General Bursar of the Society of Saint Pius X, a post which he still occupies.

Throughout the central and essential part of the new bishop's consecration, while a headband and sling protect the Holy Chrism on his head and hands, a Missal representing the Gospels is laid across his neck and back. His essential burden will be to preach the Gospel.

The new bishop's hands are anointed with Holy Chrism. The crown of his head will also be anointed. Hence the headband, in case the Holy Chrism were to overflow!

Fr. Richard Williamson (below) received a Degree from the University of Cambridge, and devoted more than seven years to teaching literature, an activity which took him for two years to the heart of black Africa. At 30, he abjured Anglicanism and converted to the Catholic Faith. In October 1972 he entered the seminary in Ecône and was ordained in 1976. He has succesively been a professor at Society seminaries in Germany and Ecône, and since 1983 has been Rector of the North American seminary of the Society, now located in Winona, Minnesota.

The rings on their right hands show that the four priests are already bishops. At a side altar they are celebrating the first part of the Mass. At the main altar behind they will celebrate with the consecrating bishop the remainder of the Mass.

New Bishop Fellay, with the tonsure for anointing clearly visible on the crown of his head, presents a loaf of bread to the bishop who has just consecrated him. Each new bishop presents to the consecrator loaves, wine and candles at the moment of the Offertory in the consecration Mass.

"Take heed to yourselves, and to the whole flock, wherein the Holy Ghost hath placed you bishops, to rule the Church of God, which He hath purchased with His own blood" (*Acts* 20:28).

"For a bishop must be without crime, as the steward of God: not proud, not subject to anger, not given to wine, no striker, not greedy of filthy lucre: but given to hospitality, gentle, sober, just, holy, continent: embracing that faithful word which is according to doctrine, that he may be able to exhort in sound doctrine, and to convince the gainsayers" (*Titus* 1:7-10).

"Feed the flock of God which is among you, taking care of it, not by constraint, but willingly, according to God:..." (*1 Peter* 5:2).

Close to the end of the ceremony of their consecration, the new bishops are enthroned before the main altar.

Fr. Tissier de Mallerais (left) was born in Sallanches (upper Savoy), in France. In 1969 he entered the seminary of St. Pius X, then in Fribourg, Switzerland. He was ordained a priest at Ecône on June 29, 1975, was appointed professor there and named Rector from 1979 to 1983. For a short time he was chaplain of the Novitiate of the Sisters of the Society of Saint Pius X at St. Michel-en-Brenne, in France. In 1984 he was elected General Secretary of the Society of Saint Pius X, a post which he holds to this day.

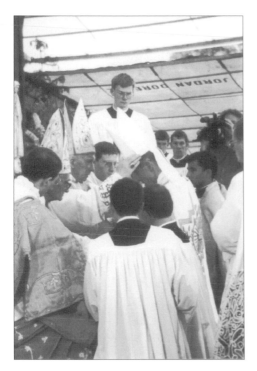

Archbishop Lefebvre, closely watched by his co-consecrator Bishop de Castro Mayer, places the mitre on the new bishop's head, while he prays "...through this armor for his head may he be for the enemies of the truth a sight terrible to behold with the double strength of Old and New Testaments, and may he mightily overwhelm them, with the help of Thy grace, O Lord, who didst crown the face of thy servant Moses bright from conversing with Thee, with brilliant horns of light and truth, and who didst order a tiara to be placed on the head of thy servant Aaron..."

Argentinian *Fr. Alfonso de Galarreta* began his priestly training in a diocesan seminary. Realizing that the formation being given there no longer corresponded to the ideal of the priesthood as the Church has always understood it, Fr. de Galarreta entered the seminary of Ecône in 1978. He was ordained by Archbishop Lefebvre in 1980. From 1980 to 1985 he was professor at the Society's seminary at la Reja in Argentina, after which he was nominated superior of the South American District, whose territory is the most extensive in the Society of Saint Pius X.

"I am simply a bishop...who is continuing to transmit Catholic doctrine. I think, and this will certainly not be too far off, you will be able to engrave on my tombstone these words of St. Paul: *Tradidi quod et accepi*–I have transmitted to you what I have received."

From left to right, in white vestments: Bishop Alfonso de Galarreta, Bishop Bernard Tissier de Mallerais (Bishop Antonio de Castro Mayer, Archbishop Marcel Lefebvre), Bishop Richard Williamson, Bishop Bernard Fellay.

General Council of Superiors of the Society of Saint Pius X, Ecône, Switzerland, July 1988.

His statements are inbred with fear, not a fear of isolation and timidity, but a fear of urgency. Assess his various comments over the last three decades:

September 1976: You cannot marry truth and error, because that is like adultery, and the child will be a bastard — a bastard rite for Mass, bastard sacraments and bastard priest.[175]

July 1977: The Church is full of thieves, mercenaries and wolves. During the past 20 years, the Vatican has become the friend of our enemies.[176]

November 1977: [Though] the Pope is angry with us. . . [he] is not very strongly against us because if he were he would excommunicate us.[177]

January 1979: Why should I give up the truth? It is Rome that is wrong, not I.[178]

December 1987: But, I can assure you, Rome, witnessing these benefits of our resistance to Modernism and our fidelity to the Catholic Faith, should logically help us to maintain this Catholic Faith. If, God forbid, they should ask us to make a compromise with the errors of the Council, since there are many high-ranking Roman personalities who do not acknowledge that today's bad fruits have their roots in the Council itself, then we will not be able to accept them. Indeed, it is clear to us that all the fruits of this new Pentecost are far from being a cause of joy for the Church, they

175 Merrill Shells & Jane Friedman, *Defiant Archbishop*, Newsweek (Sept. 13, 1976).
176 Note, *The Church is Full of Wolves*, Time 64 (July 11, 1977).
177 George A. Kelly, *The Battle for the American Church*, 417 (1979).
178 George A. Kelly, *The Battle for the American Church*, 417 (1979).

are poisoned. Thus, if they absolutely want us to make a compromise with these "modernist" doctrines, that are destroying our Faith, we will refuse; we want to remain Catholic; we have not been fighting for twenty years against these errors in order to abandon our fight, and then join with the ranks of those who are losing the Faith.[179]

June 1, 1988: Excommunicated by whom? By modernists, by people who should themselves be publicly excommunicated. It has no value.[180]

September 1990: So, they are no small errors. We are not dealing in trifles. We are into a line of philosophical thinking that goes back to Kant, Descartes, the whole line of modern philosophers who paved the way for the revolution.[181]

Unquestionably, this discourse exposes a mentality of fear, of grave concern over the state of Catholicism. These ruminations are not cavalier points of debate, but an intellectual earnestness intent on withstanding a continuing ecclesiastical disintegration. From the Archbishop's viewpoint, the Church is in a state of emergency. To consecrate is the only choice, since the author of the mandate, the Pope, breaches Lefebvre's traditional and unified view of Catholic life, tradition and heritage. Coriden, Green and Heintschel ascribe a certain relativity to fear that even the dear Archbishop could rely upon.

---

179 Marcel Lefebvre, No Compromise with Modernist Doctrines, Letters to Friends and Benefactors 4 (The Society of Saint Pius X, ed., Mar. 1988).
180 Richard N. Ostling, *The Archbishop Calls it Quits*, Time 43 (June 27, 1988).
181 Marcel Lefebvre, Two Years After the Consecration — We must Not Waiver, We May Not Compromise, Archbishop Lefebvre's address to his priests, 6 (September 6, 1990).

Likewise impaired in his or her decisional process is the person who acts out of grave fear, even if it is only relative, i.e., sufficient to intimidate the alleged offender even if not all persons.[182]

Even if the argument is lost as to extinguished imputability, the Archbishop could raise rightfully an argument of diminished imputability. The 1983 Code's aversion to sanctions and penalties makes diminished imputability a likely happenstance. Even if there was harm to souls, the minimization argument has merit.

Canon 1324 at §8 allows the actor even to think erroneously. Cross-referencing Canon 1323 §4 and 5, the 1983 Code Canon 1324 permits a diminution of imputability if the actor's conviction was wrongly based on legitimate fear and necessity. Even in the worst of settings, the Archbishop's *latae sententiae* penalty would have been mitigated because he feared certain results, whether it be the collapse of the Church or a loss of faith. The Italian newsletter *SiSi NoNo* labels the times of Lefebvre "extraordinary".

Uneasiness amongst the faithful is the consequence. They find themselves attacked in the Faith by those very people who should be their guardians and their teachers, and find themselves conscience-bound to resist those whom they would wish, and in normal times would have the duty, to follow as pastors. Uneasiness also follows among those bishops who feel in conscience the duty of resisting (that they do not do so, for various reasons, is a different matter)

182 James A. Coriden, Thomas J. Green, Donald E. Heintschel, The Code of Canon Law A Text and Commentary 902 (1990).

authority, which has the duty of ensuring unity of government in the Church, authority with whom they would be, and in normal times should be, in communion. This "extraordinary" situation in the Church imposes, over and above, extraordinary duties on all.[183]

Father Fernando Rifan, by logical extension, finds necessity in not only a supply of traditional priests but in the fruition of their sacramental authority:

1. Nécessité	1. Necessity
Devant la crise actuelle sans précédent dans l'histoire de l'Eglise, crise de la Foi et de la Morale ; devant le progressisme qui n'est pas autre chose que le Modernisme installé jusqu'aux plus hauts postes de l'Eglise ; devant la lamentable apostasie généralisée des prêtres et des évêques, il est de la plus nécessité et de la plus grand urgence d'avoir des évêques fidèles à la Tradition.	Before the actual crisis which is without precedent in the history of the Church, a crisis of Faith and Ethics; before progressiveness, which is nothing but modernism installed to the highest posts of the Church; before the lamentable general apostasy of the priests and the bishops, it is of the highest necessity and the greatest urgency to have bishops who are true to the Tradition.
Nécessité, pour la garde et la transmission pure et intègre du dépôt de la Foi et pour l'ordination de prêtres qui garantissent la continuité du Saint Sacrifice de la messe et des Sacrements.	Necessity, for the keeping and the pure and integral transmission of the deposit of the Faith and for ordination of the priests who guarantee the continuity of the Holy Sacrifice of the Mass and of the Sacraments.
Urgence, parce que cela fait plus de vingt ans que cette crise dure sans aucune perspective de changement de la part des autorités actuelles: il est impossible d'attendre davantage.[184]	Urgency, because it is already more than twenty years that this crisis exists, without any perspective of change on the part of the actual authorities: it is impossible to wait any longer.[185]

183 Courrier de Rome *Neither Schismatic Nor Excommunicated* in Is Tradition Excommunicated? Where is Catholicism Today? 1, 18-19 (The Society of Saint Pius X, ed., Mar. 1993).
184 Fernando Arêas Rifan, Eclaircissements sur les sacres conférés par S. Exc. Marcel Lefebvre 1 (1990).
185 Fernando Arêas Rifan, Eclaircissements sur les sacres conférés par S. Exc. Marcel Lefebvre 1 (1990).

But is a man as experienced as Marcel Lefebvre so easily moved by fear? Can the will of a man of stern belief and ideas be influenced so readily? Can violence be exerted against the will of Lefebvre? Canonist McCoy judges with rigor:

> Such moral violence by which the will is forced to place some act which is materially or of its own objectiveness criminal, can be effected by the mis-guided dictate either of reason or of the sensitive appetency. It is occasioned by the sensitive appe-tency when the object of the volition, which is in itself and ontologically a bad object, is represented to the will as a good object inasmuch as the indwelling propensities of the senses prevail over the enlight-ened dictates of reason. This is the case when the will is moved to a criminal act under the influence of passion. The moral violence to the will is occasioned by reason when the object of the volition which is otherwise evil, and hence despicable, appears as an object that is good and hence desirable, because of the concurrence of certain circumstances. This is the case when a man sees himself in a state of so-called "con-ditional necessity". In such circumstances, he finds it impossible to avoid a threatened evil, or to defend his rights, or to fulfill his legal duties, unless he places an act which is materially criminal (*in se spectatus*).[186]

Lefebvre's very conviction, its intensity, and sincerity make fear a likely companion: Fear exists because he truly appreciated the way things were and are.

---

186 Alan E. McCoy, Force and Fear in Relation to Delictual Imputability and Penal Responsibility 75 (1944).

LEGAL HOLDING 3.1: That under the Code of 1917, fear, whether grave or slight, will neither remove nor diminish imputability for the act of consecration by the Archbishop Marcel Lefebvre was listed as damaging to the salvation of souls at Canon 2205 and 2229.

LEGAL HOLDING 3.2: That under the Code of 1983 grave fear, and even relative fear, as manifested by his action and word, will remove imputability for his actions, if they do no harm to souls as enunicated at Canon 1323, 4°.

LEGAL HOLDING 3.3: That under the Code of 1983, at Canon 1324, 5°, 8° and 10°, the *latae sententiae* excommunication if declared valid, would be diminished or mitigated by the existence of fear.

CHAPTER 8

Necessity and Imputability

LEGAL ISSUE #4: Whether necessity can excuse or mitigate the Archbishop's imputability for the unauthorized act
of consecration.

I. The Nature of Necessity

In some canonical circles, there is little difference between grave fear and necessity. The concepts, however,
though aligned, are foundationally different. In both the
1917 and 1983 Code, *necessitas*, as well as grave inconvenience *(grave incommodum)*, provide a similar avenue of challenge as fear:

Canon 2205. - §2. Metus quoque gravis, etiam relative tantum, *necessitas*, imo et grave incommodum, plerumque delictum, si agatur de legibus mere ecclesiasticis, penitus tollunt.[187]	Canon 2205. - §2 Grave fear, even though only relatively such, *necessity*, and even great inconvenience, excuse as a rule from all liability, if there is question of purely ecclesiastical laws.[188]

---

187 Code of Canon Law, Canon 2205, §2 (1917).
188 Stanislaus Woywod, A Practical Commentary on the Code of Canon Law, 452
    (2952).

Canon 1323 - 4° metu gravi, quamvis relative tantum, coactus egit, aut ex necessitate vel gravi incommodo, nisi tamen actus sit intrinsece malus aut vergat in animarum damnum;[189]

Canon 1323 - 4° a person who acted out of grave fear, even if only relatively grave, or out of necessity or out of serious inconvenience unless the act is intrinisically evil or verges on harm to souls;[190]

Necessity can always mitigate the penalty:

Canon 1324 - 5° ab eo, qui metu gravi, quamvis relative tantum, coactus est, aut ex necessitate vel gravi incommodo, si delictum sit intrinsece malum vel in animarum damnum vergat;[191]

Canon 1324 - 5° by a person who was forced through grave fear, even if only relatively grave, or through necessity or serious inconvenience, if the offense was intrinsically evil or verged on harm to souls;[192]

Necessity arises from the state of things. In necessity, things are done because they have to be done to insure one's rights. Necessity is a product of free will. "Grave hardship" (*grave incommodum*) is relative necessity of moral impossibility. Canonists consider the role of fear from within (*ab intrinseco*), that is, both the fear arising from an interior cause and also the fear arising from a necessary exterior cause, under the heading of necessity and grave hardship."[193]

Necessity is either physical or spiritual in nature. "Spiritual necessity is that which thrusts the agent into the position of necessarily having to choose between some harm to his own soul or the souls of others and the violation of some penal law."[194]

---

189 Code of Canon Law, Canon 1323, 4° (1983).
190 Code of Canon Law, Canon 1323, 4° (1983).
191 Code of Canon Law, Canon 1324, 5° (1983).
192 Code of Canon Law, Canon 1324, 5° (1983).
193 Alan E. McCoy, Force and Fear in Relation to Delictual Imputability and Penal Responsibility 84 (1944).
194 Alan E. McCoy, Force and Fear in Relation to Delictual Imputability and Penal Responsibility 84 (1944).

Necessity is further devised into degrees or extremes, from grave to slight. In the matter before us, the strained and ambivalent character of the Church, in the Lefebvre view, represents grave circumstances. Grave necessity opens the door to extraordinary means.

II. Necessity and the Archbishop

As to the Archbishop, the doctrine of necessity would be argued as follows:

1. Canon 1382 prohibits consecration without papal mandate.
2. The Archbishop sees his own health at risk.
3. The Archbishop desires to continue his order, the Priestly Society of Saint Pius X.
4. The Archbishop has thousands of souls unserved by traditional sacraments and Mass.
5. The Archbishop believes the only salvation is a return to tradition previous to Vatican II and its pastoral teachings.
6. The Archbishop is constantly badgered by Vatican authorities.
7. The Archbishop knows without Bishops, there will be no priests.

To invoke necessity, the claimant need show the action has legitimacy despite the law. *Necessitas non habet legem* — necessity has no law — is the defense's underlying theme.

These requirements aside, does the Archbishop provide a suitable and substantive basis for the necessity defense? Arriving at a judgment in this matter is largely discretionary since both Codes do not lay out factual circumstances that encompass *necessitas* or *grave incommodum*. Canonist Dr. Georg May portrays these discretionary parameters:

The law does not say what is meant by this item; it leaves to jurisprudence and doctors the task of giving it a precise meaning. But it is clear from the context that necessity is a state wherein goods necessary for life are put in danger in such a way to come out of this state the violation of certain laws is inevitable.[195]

This being so, what reasonable interpretation could an arbiter give to the Archbishop's necessity defense? Oratorian canonist Glover is satisfied by the Archbishop's perceived and actual belief that he needs priests to save souls and to assure the traditional order:

Again, it is clear that it was the necessity of providing for a future supply of traditional priests which caused the Archbishop and his co-consecrator to act as they did, after all hope for a "reconciliation" with Rome had proved groundless.[196]

L'abbé Gérard Mura's recent work, *Les Sacres Episcopaux de 1988* integrates the necessity argument into his central thesis that higher laws of the Church make the Archbishop's action legal:

---

195 Georg May, *The Disposition of Law in Case of Necessity Within the Church*, Is Tradition Excommunicated? Where is Catholicism Today? 111 (Society of Saint Pius X, ed., 1993).
196 T.C.G. Glover, *Schism and Archbishop Lefebvre* in Is Tradition Excommunicated? Where is Catholicism Today? 97, 98 (Society of Saint Pius X, ed., 1993).

Pour finir, précisons que le fil conducteur de ce travail et ses idées directrices se retrouvent dans le "Mandat apostolique" qui a été lu lors des sacres. On y mentionne l'esprit moderniste qui inspire les autorités de l'Église romaine et on démontre l'état de nécessité qui a atteint les sommets de l'Église. C'est pourquoi on déclare les peines et les censures décrétées par ces autorités nulles et non avenues, dans la mesure où les dignitaires ecclésiastiques agissent contre les saintes traditions et donc contre le salut des âmes, fin suprême et bien commun de l'Église. On rappelle que l'exigence du mandat pontifical a son origine dans l'obligation que chaque évêque a reçue de l'Église de transmettre à tous les hommes, pour le salut de leurs âmes, les traditions venues des Apôtres. Et on souligne que la cérémonie des sacres prévoit de faire appel à l'avis des fidèles qui ont un droit au "pain de vie, le Christ ".[197]

To end, let's remark that the conducting thread of this work and its direct ideas can be found in the "Mandate Apostolique" - apostolic mandate, which has been read at the time of the consecrations. Therein is mentioned the modernistic spirit which inspires the authorities of the Roman Church and a state of necessity is shown, which has reached the summit of the Church. This is why one declares the troubles and decreed censures of the authorities to be null and void, to the point where the dignitaries of the Church act against the holy traditions, and thus against the salvation of the souls, the highest goal and common good of the Church. One is reminded that the requirement of the papal mandate has its origin in the obligation that each bishop has received from the Church, to transmit, to all people, for the salvation of their souls, the traditions which came from the Apostles. And one underlines that the ceremony of the consecrations foresees making appeal to the true believers who have a right to the "bread of life, the Christ".[198]

Mura labels the Church situation one of "grave emergency" and that any action that *saves souls* in this current malaise is necessitous. He further remarks:

197 Gérald Mura, *Les sacres épiscopaux de 1988, Etude théologique (I)*, 4 Le Sel De La Terre 27, 44-45 (1993).
198 Gérald Mura, *Les sacres épiscopaux de 1988, Etude théoligique (I)*, 4 Le Sel De La Terre 27, 44-45 (1993).

C'est pourquoi le code de droit canonique publié en 1983 rappelle très opportunément dans son ultime canon que "le salut des âmes est la loi suprême". Si l'interdiction des sacres épisopaux sans mandat pontifical est purement humaine et canonique et va, dans le cas qui nous intéresse, contre la gloire de Dieu et le salut des âmes, il est évident que l'objection tombe d'elle-même.[199]

This is why the canonical law code published in 1983, quite opportunistically brings to mind in its ultimate canon that "the salvation of souls is the supreme law". If the interdiction of the consecrations of the bishops without pontifical mandate is purely human and canonical and goes, in the case which interests us, against the glory of God and the sanctification of the souls, it is evident that the objection falls down on its own.[200]

Does necessity require a more objective measure aside from the grim view of modern Catholicism? Does a paucity of traditional priests and their sacramental function meet the burden? Doesn't necessity require a crisis mentality, a mentality that forces us to do a wrong in order to avoid an even greater error? Was the Pope's sloth-like response to requests to consecrate a basis for necessity? Francois Pivert can live without the crisis and the Pope's recalcitrance to find necessity. For Pivert, any obstacle that impedes the building of the Church creates a necessitous reality:

Il n'est pas nécessaire d'analyser toute la crise de l'Église, pour constater que Jean-Paul II s'oppose de fait à la survie de l'épiscopat traditionnel. Si vraiment il n'en voulait qu'à Mgr Lefebvre et non à ce que celui-ci représente, le Pape nommerait en dehors de la Fraternité, au moins quelques évêques traditionalistes.[201]

It's not necessary to analyze the whole crisis in the Church, to see that John Paul II opposes the traditional episcopate. If he really didn't want Mgr. Lefebvre and those he represents, the Pope should at least have nominated several traditionalist bishops outside the Society.[202]

199 Gérald Mura, *Les sacres épiscopaux de 1988, Etude théologique (I)*, 4 Le Sel De La Terre 27, 29 (1993).
200 Gérald Mura, *Les sacres épiscopaux de 1988, Etude théologique (I)*, 4 Le Sel De La Terre 27, 29 (1993).
201 François Pivert, *Des Sacres Par Mgr. Lefebvre. . . Un Schisme?* 32 (1988).
202 François Pivert, *Des Sacres Par Mgr. Lefebvre. . . Un Schisme?* 32 (1988).

Par conséquent le Pape n'aurait pas le pouvoir de lier Mgr Lefebvre (en l'excommuniant par exemple) pour l'empêcher de construire l'Église : il est bien obligé d'admettre la juridiction, limitée certes mais réelle, que Notre Seigneur et l'Église transmettent sans lui, en vertu du droit qui lui est supérieur.[203]

Consequently, the Pope doesn't have the power to tie down Mgr. Lefebvre (by excommunicating) to keep him from building the Church: the double affirmation of Our Lord (I'll build...all that you will build...) teaches us that who is not tied to the Pope doesn't build the Church, but also that whoever builds the Church is necessarily by right tied to the Pope as he also builds the Church.[204]

Using this line of reasoning, Pivert and other supporters of the Archbishop, find the case and circumstance of Marcel Lefebvre analogous to Christians in the Roman coliseum. While the lions caused grave inconvenience to the physical being of Christians, so too the Archbishop and his followers, are in a severe state of spiritual annihilation. Pivert remarks:

On aura remarqué que ce canon est très large avec les termes "grave inconvénient". Il peut s'agir d'un grave inconvénient physique: par exemple, difficulté à se déplacer sur une longue distance en pays de mission pour rejoindre le missionnarie ; ou moral : risque de faire repérer le prêtre en temps de persécution.[205]

We shall have seen that this canon is very stretchable regarding the term "grave inconvenience". It may be a severe physical condition: e.g. difficulty to move over long distances in mission countries to rejoin the missionary; or moral: risk to have the priest "marked" in times of persecution.[206]

Spiritual life is on par with physical life. Canonist McGrath comments:

The inability to obey the law is extrinsic to the agent, and is the result of causes such as nature, or the lack of means necessary for life.[207]

---

203 François Pivert, Des Sacres Par Mgr Lefebvre. . . Un Schisme? 36 (1988).
204 François Pivert, Des Sacres Par Mgr Lefebvre. . . Un Schisme? 36 (1988).
205 François Pivert, Des Sacres Par Mgr Lefebvre. . . Un Schisme? 22 (1988).
206 François Pivert, Des Sacres Par Mgr Lefebvre. . . Un Schisme? 22 (1988).
207 John J. McGrath, Comparative Study of Crime and its Imputability in Ecclesiastical Criminal Law and in America Criminal Law 47, 67 (1957).

Pivert cites the parties seeking marriage bonds as typical of the modern crisis:

Dans les circonstances actuelles, les fiancés se trouvent confrontés principalement à trois graves inconvénients : la nouvelle messe, le laxisme moral des prêtres et leur laxisme doctrinal.[208]	Under the actual circumstances, the betrothed are confronted principally by three serious matters of inconvenience: The New Mass, the lax morality of the priests and their laxism in doctrine.[209]

Canonist McCoy refers to the state where necessity is justified as "moral powerlessness."

In penal law, necessity may be defined as the objective condition of things, brought about in any manner whatsoever, in which an act that according to penal law is to be placed or omitted cannot be so placed or omitted because of an absolute or moral powerlessness, whether this latter be physical or spiritual.[210]

Whether this crisis is factually or theologically justified is another matter all together. For canonical purposes, that debate is really irrelevant since the 1983 Code grants the defense to those who believe them to be true. Thus, if a man believes only the Traditional Latin Mass fulfills the weekly obligation, his frame of reference will resist the new Mass at all costs. Thus, if a man judges ecumenism as antithetical to Catholic philosophy and theology, his resistance to Vatican II's pastoral teachings will be contrary by necessity. If that same man weighs a collapse of priestly vocations, a thorough demise of seminary enrollment and dwindling Church attendance as signs of crisis, he will act to contain these results by

---

208 François Pivert, Des Sacres Par Mgr Lefebvre. . . Un Schisme? 22 (1988).
209 François Pivert, Des Sacres Par Mgr Lefebvre. . . Un Schisme? 22 (1988).
210 Alan E. McCoy, Force and Fear in Relation to Delictual Imputability and Penal Responsibility 83 (1944).

necessitous means. To Lefebvre, without bishops, the crisis triggering spiritual necessity would grow a thousand-fold. Even the staunchest of the Archbishop's critics will admit the Church is not what it used to be. Radical feminists worship mother-nature and New-Ageism; moral theology and philosophy have too much proportionalism; a lame episcopacy, and a pedophilic and homosexual invasion in the ranks of the priesthood all signify the turmoil. These states are objective factors in the determination of crisis — not sentimental antagonism. One would have to have one's head buried in sand to not witness the inculcation of secularism, materialism, feminism, and other ideas of the radical chic into the Church proper. Is it not reasonable to conclude that the Church is in crisis? Canonist Kaschewsky sees the 1983 Code's necessity criteria as an infallible defense for the Archbishop:

Fassen wir zusammen:

a) Wegen Vorliegens einer echten Notlage trifft den Spender einer Bischofsweihe ohne päpstlichen Auftrag unter den geschilderten Umständen keine Strafe (Can. 1323 Nr. 4).

b) Auch wenn die Notlage objektiv nicht vorliegen würde, bliebe der "Täter" dennoch straffrei, weil er schuldlos subjektiv der Meinung war, diese Notlage habe vorgelegen (Can. 1324 §1 Nr. 5).

c) Auch wenn die irrige Annahme des Vorhandenseins einer Notlage verschuldet wäre, so würde dennoch keine Tatstrafe und erst recht keine Exkommunikation eintreten (Can. 1324 §1 Nr. 8, §3)[211]

Summarizing:

a) Because of an existing state of emergency, the given of an episcopal consecration without papal order is not punishable under these circumstances (Can. 1324 No. 4).

b) Even if this state of emergency would objectively not exist, the perpetrator remains free from punishment, because he was subjectively of the opinion that this state of emergency existed (Can. 1324 §1 No.5).

c) Also, if the erroneous belief of the existence of state of emergency carried guilt, even then there would follow *no* punishment and certainly not excommunication (Can. 1324 §1 No. 8, §3).[212]

---

211 Von Rudolf Kaschewsky, *Zur Frage der Bishchofsweihe ohne Päpstlichen Auftrag*, Vra Voce Korrespontenz 86, 90-91 (sum. 1988).
212 Von Rudolf Kaschewsky, *Zur Frage der Bischofsweihe ohne Päpstlichen Auftrag*, Vra Voce Korrespontenz 86, 90-91 (sum. 1988).

Hence, accepting the Archbishop's perception of the Church, his choice to consecrate without papal mandate was made necessitously. As canonist McGrath offers:

> Grave hardship involves a relative powerlessness for the fulfillment of the law. One can indeed fulfill the law, but only at the price of a hardship which the legislator does not intend that one should suffer for the sake of a compliance with his law.[213]

Dr. Georg May corroborates this element:

> The Church, and in first place its organs, has the right but also the duty of taking all the measures necessary for the removal of dangers. In a situation of necessity the pastors of the Church can take extraordinary measures to protect or re-establish the activity of the Church. If an organ does not carry out its necessary or indispensable functions, the other organs have the duty and the right to use the power they have in the Church so that the life of the Church is guaranteed and its end attained. If the authorities of the Church refuse this, the responsibility of other members of the Church increases, but also their juridical competence.[214]

LEGAL HOLDING 4.1: That under the Code of 1917, the Archbishop's action of consecration would not be justified by necessity since his action was in

---

213 John J. McGrath, Comparative Study of Crime and its Imputability in Ecclesiastical Criminal Law and in America Criminal law 47, 67 (1957).
214 Georg May, *The Disposition of Law in Case of Necessity within the Church*, Is Tradition Excommunicated? Where is Catholicism Today?, 111, 112-13 (Society of Saint Pius X, ed., 1993).

contempt of Church authorities and listed as an offense causing damage to souls under Canons 2205 and 2229.

LEGAL HOLDING 4.2: That under the Code of 1983, the act of consecration would be justified by necessity given the state of the Church and remove all imputability since his action did not "verge on harm to souls" under Canon at 1323, 4°.

LEGAL HOLDING 4.3: That under the Code of 1983, the act of consecration would not result in full imputability since the agent believed he was justified by the current state of the Church under Canon 1324 4°, 5° and 10°.

CHAPTER 9

Schism

LEGAL ISSUE #5: Whether the Archbishop's act of consecration, without papal mandate, is an act of formal schism.

I. The Decree of Schism in the Case of Marcel Lefebvre

In decreeing the excommunication of the Archbishop, the Pope and the Congregation of Bishops enhanced the penalty by declaring him a *"schismatic."* By less than canonical logic, the Pope in *Ecclesia Dei Afflicta* correlated an act of disobedience to an act of schism. The Pope so held:

> Hence, such disobedience — which implies in practice the rejection of the Roman primacy — constitutes a schismatic act.[216]

The Latin bears no different interpretation:

> Quam ob rem talis inoboedientia — secum quae infert vera repudiatio Primatus Romani — actum *schismaticum* efficit.[217]

---

216 Note, *The Apostolic Letter Ecclesia Dei*, Inside the Vatican 20 (Aug./Sept. 1993).
217 Note, *Lo Scisma Di Lefebvre*, LXI Apollinaris 529, 547 (1988).

The Pope's *motu proprio* further references the notion of schism at paragraph 4:

Huius autem schismatic actus *radix* dignosci potest in ipsa aliqua imperfecta et pugnanti sibi notione Traditionis. . .[218]	The root of this schismatic act can be discerned in an incomplete and contradictory notion of Tradition.[219]

On July 1, 1988, Prefect of the Congregation of Bishops issued a *Decree* supportive of the Pope's allegations. Cardinal Gantin so states:

> Monsignor Marcel Lefebvre, formerly Archbishop-Bishop of Tulle, despite a formal warning on 17th June and repeated attempts to persuade him to renounce his resolve has committed a schismatic act by consecrating as Bishops four priests without papal mandate and against the express wish of the Holy Father and thereby has incurred the penalties laid down by Canon 1364 para 1 and Canon 1382 of the Code of Canon Law.
>
> I declare that in accordance with these laws the above mentioned Archbishop Marcel Lefebvre, Bernard Fellay, Bernard Tissier de Mallerais, Richard Williamson and Alfonso de Galarreta have *ipso facto* incurred excommunication *latae sententiae* reserved to the Holy See.
>
> Furthermore, I declare that Monsignor Antonio de Castro Mayer, retired Bishop of Campos, having directly participated in the ceremony as co-consecrator and having publicly involved himself in an act of schism has incurred excommunication *latae sententiae* as laid down by Canon 1364 §1.

---

218 Note, *Ecclesia Dei*, 61 Acta Appotolicae Sedis 547 (1988).
219 Note, *The Apostolic Letter Ecclesia Dei*, Inside the Vatican 20 (Aug./Sept. 1993).

Priests and laity are warned not to give allegiance
to the schism initiated by Archbishop Lefebvre lest
they incur the same penalty of excommunication.
From the Congregation of Bishops, 1st July 1988
Bernardin Cardinal Gantin
Prefect[220]

On two counts, Cardinal Gantin imposed penalties *latae sententiae*: the first being Canon 1382 on unlawful consecration, and second, an act of schism under Canon 1364.

Within Cardinal Gantin's decree is the extraordinary warranty that these same penalties are imposed, by implication, on anyone supportive to this schismatic movement. What does this really mean? To have allegiance to the bishops consecrated? Or, does it follow that any and all activities of the Archbishop and his Priestly Society conjure up schism? Is the Latin Mass inherently schismatic? Is it schismatic to donate dollars to a Lefebvre cause? By what canonical authority can allegiance be demonstrated?

On July 30, 1990, the Congregation of Faith, in correspondence with Bishop Joseph Candalfi, responded to a query on the Society:

---

220 Note, *Archbishop Lefebvre, The Time for Decision*, 75 Canon Law Society, Great Britain & Ireland Newsletter 14, 47 (1988).

En réponse, ce Dicastère vous confirme que les membres de la Fraternité Saint-Pie X, vu qu'ils ont suivi Mgr Marcel Lefebvre après son acte schismatique du 30 juin 1988, ne peuvent plus être considérés comme faisant partie de l'Eglise catholique romaine, ceci conformément à l'avertissement contune dans le dernier paragraphe du Décret porté par la Congrégation pour les Evêques le 1 juillet 1988 (cf. Annexe), et en vertu des dispositions des canon 751 et 1364 du Code de Droit Canonique.[221]	In reply, this "Dicastory" confirms to you that the members of the Society of Pius X, as they have followed Mgr. Lefebvre after his schismatic act of June 30, 1988, cannot any longer be considered to belong to the Roman Catholic Church, and this conforms to the announcement in the last paragraph of the Decree carried by the Congregation of the Bishops of July 1, 1988, and based on the dispositions of Canons 751 and 1364 of the Canon Law Code.[222]

How the Congregation defines "follows" is open to suggestion.

English primate Cardinal Hume, on June 16, 1988, mused on the canonical implications of the act of consecration:

Those who are sympathetic to Archbishop Lefebvre and may have found it almost impossible to accept the renewal of Church life endorsed by the Second Vatican Council are now faced with a painful choice. I would urge them to reaffirm their loyalty to the Successor of St. Peter and to remain within the unity of the Catholic Church. To continue in support of the Archbishop and to worship with the Fraternity of St. Pius X is to leave the Catholic Church. It has always been my firm belief that a full understanding of the implications of the Second Vatican Council is going to take a long time. The process has necessarily been slow and not without difficulties, especially where the liturgy is concerned.[223]

221 Letter to Joseph Candolfi from Joseph Ratzinger, July 30, 1990.
222 Letter to Joseph Candolfi from Joseph Ratzinger, July 30, 1990.
223 Note, *Archbishop Lefebvre, The Time for Decision*, 75 Canon Law Society, Great Britain & Ireland Newsletter 14, 38 (1988).

Some interesting propositions emerge in Hume's commentary. Is dissent schism? Is the demand for traditional Mass and sacraments schismatic? When, if ever, did Marcel Lefebvre question the faith and moral authority of the papacy? Is it schismatic to resist an infusion of the secular world into the Church? Is it schismatic to oppose ecumenism? By any legal standard, Cardinal Hume's conclusions are specious. Proclaiming schism is dramatically different than proving it. Let's purge the obvious emotions spewed forth by this prelate and stick to the Code.

II. The Code of 1917: Schism

Schism has been historically known as a rejection of hierarchical authority with the intent to establish a parallel Church. Canon 1325 §2 of the 1917 Code, after its discussion of heresy and apostasy, defines schism:

Canon 1325 - §2. Post receptum baptismum si quis, nomen retinens christianum, pertinaciter aliquam ex veritatibus fide divina et Catholica credendis denegat aut de ea dubitat, haereticus; si a fide christiana totaliter recedit, apostata; si denique subesse renuint Summo Pontifici aut cum membris Ecclesiae ei subiectis communicare recusat, schismaticus est.[224]

Canon 1325 - §2 Any baptized person who, while retaining the name of Christian, obstinately denies or doubts any of the truths proposed for belief by the divine and Catholic faith, is a *heretic*; if he abandons the Christian faith entirely, he is called an *apostate*; if, finally, he refuses to be subject to the Supreme Pontiff, or to have communication with members of the Church subject to the Pope, he is a *schismatic*.[225]

The term schism is not equated with direct disobedience but a positive affirmation that Rome and its authorities are meaningless and unrecognized. Schism is an exercise of self-will and an attack on the unity of the Church.

---

224 Code of Canon Law, Canon 1325 §2 (1917).
225 Stanislaus Woywod, A Practical Commentary of the Code of Canon Law 108-9 (1952).

Reichel, an esteemed commentator on the 1917 Code, defines schism as:

> Schism is self-will in regard to the sacraments and consists in violating the sacrament of unity, either by setting up altar against altar or by withdrawing from communion for no adequate cause. If persisted in this, it become heresy, because it ignores the Church's note of unity, and it generally ends by inventing some new teaching to justify the separation.[226]

To find the Archbishop schismatic under the 1917 Code, the protagonist would need to outline and prove these criteria:

> 1. That by the consecrations, the Archbishop desired to leave the authority of Rome.
> 2. That by the consecrations, the Archbishop established a new Church that refused to recognize Rome.
> 3. That by the consecrations, the Archbishop refused to recognize the papacy.

In none of these circumstances can the Archbishop be found culpable. Count Neri Capponi, canonist at the University of Florence, was asked his view on the charge of schism under the 1917 Code:

> No, he would *still* not be considered a schismatic. But he would *certainly* have incurred excommunication. No ambiguity. There's a certain ambiguity day because of the allowance for extenuating circumstances.[227]

226 Oswald J. Reichel, A Complete Manual of Canon Law, 50-51 (1896).
227 Note, *Church Law, Jargon-Free and Interview with Count Neri Capponi*, 2 Latin Mass Magazine 14, 16 (May-June 1993).

Further on he is asked:

Q.   But your personal view is that there was no schism in 1988. . .?

A.   No schism, no schism in '88.[228]

At a later point he remarked:

And according to the old code also, it was not a schismatic action.   And that the excommunication itself under the rulings of the new code was certainly ambiguous.[229]

With Capponi's insight, it is difficult to see how disobedience is robotically equated with schism. Assess the direction the editors of *America* take soon after the consecration:

The reason is clear, of course. These other dissenters have never presumed to consider themselves "more Catholic than the Pope," nor have they ever directly challenged the traditional authority of the Pope, much less threatened schism. Archbishop Lefebvre, on the other hand, chose to exempt himself from the tradition of the church when he denied the authority of the Second Vatican Council. His actions are therefore very similar to those of the Old Catholics of 1870 whose very name implies that the First Vatican Council introduced into the church innovations that left Old Catholicism the repository of traditional Catholic beliefs.   Archbishop Lefebvre believes his Society of Saint Pius X is the repository

---

228 Note, *Church Law, Jargon-Free and Interview with Count Neri Capponi*, 2 Latin Mass Magazine 14, 16 (May-June 1993).
229 Note, *Church Law, Jargon-Free and Interview with Count Neri Capponi*, 2 Latin Mass Magazine 14, 16 (May-June 1993).

of traditional Catholic beliefs unsullied by the innovations of Vatican II.[230]

How does the writer arrive at this disposition logically?
Even the inexperienced historian knows the Old Catholics of
1870, those who formed a parallel Church, *The Polish National
Catholic Church*, not only disobeyed Rome but denied the
Papacy as an institution. How can one compare the Archbishop to the Rev. Stallings of Washington, D.C., who set up
a parallel, *African National Catholic Church*, defied the Papacy, and dissented from its fundamental moral teachings
on marriage, abortion and homosexuality. *These* are cases of
schism. *These* are examples of disobedience coupled with a
division in both faith and authority. *These* are not instances
of philosophical and theological dialogue and debate, but
conscious separations. In no words or deeds, in no writings
or oratory, in no orders or policy making, will the Archbishop
ever be found advocating a parallel church or the legal
irrelevancy of the Papacy.

Oratorian canonist T.C.G. Glover sees the insensibility of
the charge:

> This charge involves a large and unjustified men-
> tal leap.

> A mere act of disobedience to a superior does not
> imply denial that the superior holds office or has
> authority. The child who says, "I won't!" to his
> mother does not deny that she is his mother; the
> soldier ordered to polish his buttons by his officer,
> who instead smokes a cigarette, is not denying the
> validity of the Queen's commission.

---

230 Note, *The Renewal of Reform*, America 124, 125 (Sept. 10, 1988).

Again, for the charge of "schism" to stick, it must be certain beyond all reasonable doubt. In a word, the six bishops have not incurred excommunication for schism, so those who adhere to them cannot beexcommunicated either. There is indeed more muddled thinking here.[231]

Therefore, under the Code of 1917, the act of consecration does not manifest a refusal to recognize Rome nor set up a parallel church. At the extreme, all that can be alleged is the Archbishop may have been disobedient, though his actions may be defensible under a theory of necessity.

III. Schism: The Code of 1983

If a viable defense regarding schism exists in the Code of 1917, it is a sure bet the 1983 Code would free the Archbishop from the stated punishment and its corresponding excommunicant status. At Canon 751, in conjunction with heresy and apostasy, is the definition of schism:

Canon 751 - Dicitur haeresis, pertinax, post receptum, baptismum, alicuius veritatis fide divina et catholica credendae denegatio, aut de eadem pertinax dubitatio: apostasia, fidei christianae ex toto repudiatio; schisma, subiectionis Summo Pontifici aut communionis cum Ecclesiae membris eidem subditis detrectatio.[232]

Canon 751 - Heresy is the obstinate post-baptismal denial of some truth which must be believed with Divine and Catholic faith, or it is likewise an obstinate doubt concerning the same; apostasy is the total repudiation of the Christian faith; schism is the refusal of submission to the Roman Pontiff or of communion with the members of the Church subject to him.[233]

231 T.C.G. Glover, *Schism and Archbishop Lefebvre, Is Tradition Excommunicated? Where is Catholicism Today?*, 97, 99-100 (Society of Saint Pius X, ed., 1993).
232 Code of Canon Law, Canon 751 (1983).
233 Code of Canon Law, Canon 751 (1983).

Deduced therefrom, from its plain language, is an actor's refusal to submit to the authority of the Pope. Therein lies the dilemma. Does disobedience, justified or not, constitute a refusal to submit? Coriden, Green and Heintschel admonish canonists to construe these definitions strictly.[234]

Unbridled discretion has no place in schismatic analysis. Some canonical commentators insist that any action deemed schismatic must be performed in "bad faith".

> All of these actions, if they are to fulfill these canonical definitions, must be born of "bad faith." (Those speaking for the Commission for Revision were insistent on this point; cf. *Comm* 7:2 [1975], 150 and the *praenotanda* to the 1977 *schema*, p. 3.) Whatever else "*mala fide*" means, it is clearly the opposite of "good faith." It implies not only knowledge — that the positions taken are knowingly, consciously, and intentionally espoused, with full cognizance that they are in opposition to what is to be held "*fide divina et catholica*" — but also defiance — that the beliefs are denied or repudiated in rejection of the authority of God revealing or the church teaching.[235]

To hold one schismatic, the evidence must show an opposition to the truths of the Catholic faith. The actor must undeniably repudiate either faith or authority in the Church.

The 1983 Code enunciates various penalties for schism at Canon Law 1364:

---

234 James A. Coriden, Thomas J. Green, & Donald E. Heintschel, The Code of Canon Law, A Text and Commentary 548 (1990).
235 James A. Coriden, Thomas J. Green, & Donald E. Heintschel, The Code of Canon Law, A Text and Commentary 548 (1990).

Canon 1364 - §1. Apostata a fide, haereticus vel schismaticus in excommunicationem *latae sententiae* incurrit, firmo praescripto can. 194, §1, n. 2; clericus praeterea potest poenis, de quibus in can. 1336, §1, nn. 1, 2, et 3, puniri.

§2. Si diuturna contumacia vel scandali gravitas postulet, aliae poenae addi possunt, non excepta dimissione e statu clericali.[236]

Canon 1364 - §1. With due regard for can. 194, §1, n.2, an apostate from the faith, a heretic or a schismatic incurs automatic (*latae sententiae*) excommunication and if a cleric, he can also be punished by the penalties mentioned in can. 1336, §1, nn. 1, 2 and 3.

§2. If long lasting contumacy of the seriousness of scandal warrants it, other penalties can be added including dismissal from the clerical state.[237]

Latae sententiae excommunication occurs on two fronts in the life of the Archbishop, but the penalty's validity and enforceability of schism is an illusory charge. Coriden, Green and Heintschel, in their authoritative commentary, find the modern emphasis on pluralism, ecumenism and the like antagonistic and contradictory to heresy, apostasy and schism.

In maintaining that a *latae sententiae* penalty be incurred in these instances, Church authorities need to be sensitive to the complex issues raised by these offenses. It is difficult to determine precisely when an individual or group is guilty of apostasy, heresy, or schism according to law. This is especially true given increased theological pluralism and ecumenical contacts and confessional boundaries that are not as sharply defined as formerly. Furthermore, jurisdictional measures may be inappropriate in dealing with persons who place themselves outside of the Church. It might be better simply to declare formally an incompatibility between their faith and that of the Church. In any event, juridical certainty about the

---

236 Code of Canon Law, Canon 1364 (1983).
237 Code of Canon Law, Canon 1364 (1983).

existence and imputability of such offenses presupposes a careful inquiry into the pertinent facts.[238]

Can it be said with honesty that the Archbishop received
a *careful* inquiry into the pertinent facts? Or is it more prob-
able that the long-running feud between his ideology and
that of the Vatican II, reached its apex in this contrary act?
Editorial commentary in the *Economist* recognizes the irony
of harsh penalty in light of the age of change:

> The Roman Catholic Church opted for pluralism
> at the Second Vatican Council. Since then, it has
> correctly given much latitude to its liberals and re-
> formers, including some who say and do things the
> Pope dislikes. To push Archbishop Lefebvre out of
> the Church because he stands on the other side of
> center would violate the principle of applying the
> new pluralism evenhandedly. If the church is pre-
> pared to tolerate divergences, it should tolerate both
> sorts. The monsignori of the Vatican are nimble-wit-
> ted men. They can devise a solution which allows
> Archbishop Lefebvre to maintain his own brand of
> doubt.[239]

Count Neri Capponi winces at the cavalier use of *latae
sententiae* excommunication under a theory of schism when
questioned:

> Q.   In other words, the 1983 code does not say
> that a bishop who consecrates other bishops in defi-
> ance of the Pope is schismatic?

---

238 James A. Coriden, Thomas J. Green, & Donald E. Heintschel, The Code of
     Canon Law, A Text and Commentary 920 (1990).
239 Note, *Live With Him*, The Economist 14, 15 (July 9, 1977).

S. Thomas Aquinas

hing more. his own, it fact is that bishops in continue. do not take ng a parallel craments of hat they can

smatic. Oth-ed for in the have been all

tive and on the applies at Canon lly erroneous to per se. In other words, by its very qualification at 1382, the penalty reserved is not schism *latae sententiae* but episcopal consecration, without papal mandate, *latae sententiae* excommunication.

The Dean of the Canon Law Faculty of the Catholic Institute of Paris, Father Patrick Valdrini addresses this Vatican inclination to lump the consecration without mandate in the same genre as an act of schism.

240 Note, *Church Law, Jargon-Free and Interview with Count Neri Capponi*, 2 Latin Mass Magazine 14, 16 (May-June 1993).

In effect:

It is not the consecration of a bishop which creates
the schism, says the Dean, even if it is a grave *faux pas*
(misstep) against the discipline of the Church; what
makes the schism a fact, is to give that bishop an
apostolic mission.

For this usurpation of the powers of the Sovereign Pontiff proves that one has created a parallel
Church.[241]

Sadly, it would appear that acrimony impacted on canonical reasoning. Despite their dislike of the Archbishop,
the authorities delegated the canonical inquiry, in the matter
of Marcel Lefebvre, had an obligation to read the canonical
precepts as they are, not as they wished them to be. Catholic
author, Mary Gordon, traces an ideological, and obviously
hidden agenda the Church wields in cases of conservative
prelates:

No bishop in this century has been censured as
Lefebvre has been. Two paradoxes then emerge.
One is that the Roman Catholic Church, traditional
bastion of the Right, seems far more conformable
with the Left in this decade than it does with extreme
conservatives. The other is that the only real schism
to afflict the Church, despite the upheaval generated
by the Second Vatican Council, comes not from the
Left, not from the Dutch theologians with their Marx-
ist sympathies and their relativist stand on morals
and scriptural interpretation, but from a traditionalist French bishop who obeys too literally the *dicta* of
the past popes. Connected with this is the anomaly
that a leader of the rebellion is one whose world view

241 Note, *Question de Droit ou de confiance, L'Homme Nouveau* (17 Feb. 1988).

indicates that he values obedience to authority and connection to tradition so highly that when he sees the Church breaking with tradition he breaks with the Church.[242]

IV. Precedential Authority as to Schism

In examining this canonical case of Marcel Lefebvre, a look to precedential authority is in order.[243] How previous cases were decided illuminates the sensibility of the current decision. What does it really mean *to refuse to submit to the Roman Pontiff* in specific cases?

A. The Case of Fr. Edward McGlynn: 1887

Consider the case of the 19th century American priest Edward McGlynn, a man with a substantial following, whose avant-garde approach to liberal social justice, bordering on socialism, caught both the eye of his ordinary and Rome. From common land usage in an age of capitalism, to his promotion of individual conscience as a substitute for ecclesiastical authority, Father Edward McGlynn pressed the limits of hierarchical tolerance. During his tenure as pastor of St. Stephen's Church in New York City, McGlynn fostered his radical presence. His view of Church authority was extreme in nature. First, he qualified the priesthood and the episcopacy, in general, as deriving its power and purpose, not from the ordinary or the Pope but the laity itself.[244]

McGlynn called for a democratization of the Church:

242 Mary Gordon, *More Catholic than the Pope, Archbishop Lefebvre* and *A Romance of the One True Church,* Harper's 58, 60 (1978).
243 Paul F. Schreiber, Canonical Precedence, 115 *(1961).*
244 Michael Augustine & Robert Emmett, The Shaping of Current Catholic Conservatism on America, 1878-1902, 214 (1978).

[t]he tabor of society is not our beloved Leo but his friend George, Pontiff in a democratic Church without dominion or tiara.[245]

Any attempt to discipline McGlynn was met with his fierce resistance and a disobedient tone always flavored with Rome bashing:

I deny the right of a bishop, Propagance or Pope, to punish me for my actions as a man and a citizen... I deny their right to censure me...[246]

On June 19, 1887, McGlynn increased his attack against ecclesiastical authority:

We must distinguish between the Church and the mere administrators of what — to use an expression familiar in American politics — is the ecclesiastical, that the machine for thousands of years has been perpetrating blunders, mistakes and committing crimes...[247]

Any effort to procedurally try McGlynn was not acknow-ledged. His opposition to the Church's teaching on property ownership, confession, Catholic Schools and the authority of his superiors is felt in his diatribe against the papacy. He could not obey the Pope, he told them, because of the very religion he had learned "under the shadow of the Vatican, that a man who sins against his conscience sins against the Holy Ghost. And of even the power that sits enthroned within the Vatican commands a man to violate his con-

---

245 Michael Augustine & Robert Emmett, The Shaping of Current Catholic Conservatism on America, 1878-1902, 214-215 (1978).
246 Michael Augustine & Robert Emmett, The Shaping of Current Catholic Conservatism on America, 1878-1902, 228 (1978).
247 Michael Augustine & Robert Emmett, The Shaping of Current Catholic Conservatism on America, 1878-1902, 255 (1978).

science, to obey that command is to sin against the Holy Ghost".[248]

Robert Curran portrays McGlynn as a purveyor of Catholic counterculture that had to be checked:

He had touched off fundamental questions regarding the rights of individual conscience against ecclesiastical authority and testing to what extent the hierarchy could rightly control the lives of American Catholics, both lay and clerical.

. . .McGlynn was a threat not only because of his political and economic heterodoxy but even more so as a religious heretic and radical who seemed to be casting aside fundamental doctrines and practices of the Church epitomized in his apparent rejection of the Pope's primacy. . .[249]

Subsequent to his refusal to recant, McGlynn was excommunicated under a theory of schism. Comparatively, the McGlynn affair is instructive. McGlynn denied the Pope's primacy and authority in faith, morals and authority. Lefebvre has never denied the governance of Rome and its authority on matters of faith and morals. McGlynn believes that individual conscience supplants the Magisterium. Lefebvre would be appalled at such a theory. Human rights as McGlynn espouse are completely foreign to Lefebvre's theory of "rights". McGlynn repeatedly challenged the dogmatic teachings of the Church. Lefebvre never challenged the Church dogma.

---

248 Michael Augustine & Robert Emmett, The Shaping of Current Catholic Conservatism on America, 1878-1902, 257 (1978).
249 Michael Augustine & Robert Emmett, The Shaping of Current Catholic Conservatism on America, 1878-1902, 250 (1978).

Weighing this contrast, McGlynn is a schismatic; Lefebvre is thoroughly innocent under the allegation.

B. The Case of Givannio Taddei: 1959

Givannio Taddei, a priest in the Diocese of Biella, Italy, was ordained a priest in 1942. His admission recommendations to the priesthood were subsequently found falsified. For a period he was suspended.

In 1952 Taddei established a foundation without authorization from any ecclesiastical authority. He also engaged in positions within forbidden groups.

After preliminary discipline from his bishop, Taddei joined a non-Catholic sect and became a bishop. In 1958, he was excommunicated. He then performed ordinations, in his status as a bishop, on men who had been rejected by their lawful superiors. The priests ordained were under suspicion of heresy. Of Taddei or Lefebvre, who acted schismatically? Taddei refused to obey his bishop on direct order. Lefebvre, in the extreme case, disobeyed but with extenuating circumstances. Taddei joined a non-Catholic sect. Lefebvre remained Catholic. Taddei consecrated rejected priestly candidates under suspicion of heresy. Lefebvre ordained and consecrated non-heretical priests and bishops. Taddei does not recognize ecclesiastical authority. Lefebvre has never denied it.

In this comparison only Taddei is schismatic.[250]

C. The Case of Archbishop Ngo-dingh-Thuc: 1970

On two separate occasions , Archbishop Ngo-dingh-Thuc ordained bishops without papal mandate. In the first

---

250 James O'Connor, 8 The Canon Law Digest 720 (1963).

instance, he repented and submitted his allegiance to Rome. In the second, he declared, "*the see of Rome is vacant.*" Acting as a sedevacantist, the Archbishop ordained both priests and five bishops without approval, denying the authority of Rome.

The case of Ngo-dingh-Thuc is closely aligned to the Lefebvre instances. Both consecrated without mandate. However, despite real or excusable disobedience, only one denied the Papacy and its authority — namely Ngo-dingh-Thuc. Hence only Ngo-dingh-Thuc refused to recognize or submit himself to the Roman Pontiff.[251]

D. The Case of the Hawaii Six: 1991- 1993

Six Catholics, describing themselves as traditionalists in search for traditional Mass and Sacraments had been charged by their bishop, Joseph A. Ferrario with being schismistic. The decree and canonical monitum stated:

> Whereas on April 28, 1987, you and your accomplices established the chapel entitled, "Our Lady of Fatima" and incorporated it as a non-profit and tax exempt corporation (I.D.#6783D2) contrary to the prescriptions of Canons 205, 515.2, and 751 of the *Code of Canon Law*;
>
> Whereas, in February 1987 you produced and hosted on Radio KNDI the program, "Catholicism in Crisis", and thereafter from April 1987 until the present, continue to host and produce the aforementioned program on Radio K-108 through which you have caused grave and serious harm, namely, confusion, scandal and heresy, impugning the lawfulness and doctrinal soundness of the Roman Missal (1970)

---

251 James O'Connor, 8 *The Canon Law Digest*, 1216 (1963).

and further aligning yourselves with the Pius X schismatic movement (August 7, 1990; August 14, 1990; January 1, 1991), and acting contrary to the exhortations and admonitions of the Papal Pro-Nuncio Archbishop Pio Laghi (March 10, 1988) as well as the canons 1341, 1364.1, 1369 and 1373 of the *Code of Canon Law*;

Whereas, on May 1987 you performed a schismatic act not only procuring the services of an excommunicated Lefebvre bishop, Richard Williamson, who performed *contra iure* illicit confirmation in your chapel, but also by that very association with the aforementioned bishop incurred *ipso facto* the grave censure of excommunication as forewarned by the Office of the Congregation of Bishops at the Vatican to all the faithful (July 1, 1988);

Whereas, you did not heed the public, personal warning and admonitions of the diocesan bishop to cease and desist from your activities when he responded to you and your radio show on August 8, 1989.[252]

Employing the *latae sententiae* penalty of Canon 1364, Bishop Ferrario excommunicated these six under the principle of schism.

Succinctly put, these six Catholics sought to influence the Ferrario episcopacy by their often combative style in the advancement of pre-Vatican ways. Whether they, as individuals or a group, are prickly pears, is really not germane to the question of schism. The only question is whether or not these six Catholics deny and refuse to submit to Rome and its ecclesiastical authority.

---

252 Letter from Joseph A. Ferrario, *Bishop of Honolulu*, to Patricia Morley, (January 18, 1991).

The Bishop ordered them to cease all traditional practices:

> Therefore, I send you this formal canonical warning wherein I confirm that if you persist any further in your schismatic activities, you will, by that very fact, be subject to and declared to have incurred the most serious censure of excommunication set forth in Canon 1364 in the *Code of Canon Law*.[253]

He then implored that they stop being disobedient:

> I beseech and implore you, in the name of Christ Jesus, to cease from your pertinacious disobedience and contumacy. You have thirty (30) days to present yourself to the diocesan bishop to rectify and reconcile yourself according to the norms of Canon Law.[254]

One of the six charged with schism. Patricia Morley, formally appealed her case to the Vatican. Her eloquent discourse of February 13, 1991 is worth a read:

> I respectfully and sincerely state that I do not and have not withdrawn submission to the Holy Father nor communion with those of Christ's faithful truly subject and obedient to him. On the contrary, I protest my reverence and respect for him. With a view to purging contempt pursuant to Canon 1347(2), I do sincerely state that I am heartily sorry if someone had interpreted — albeit wrongly — any of my actions to reflect a withdrawal of submission to the Holy Father

---

253 Letter from Joseph A. Ferrario, *Bishop of Honolulu*, to Patricia Morley, (January 18, 1991).
254 Letter from Joseph A. Ferrario, *Bishop of Honolulu*, to Patricia Morley, (January 18, 1991).

or of communion with those truly subject and obedient to him.[255]

The mental leap previously referenced, that any follower of the Lefebvre movement is equally schismatic, is advanced by Ferrario in his canonical warning. Patricia Morley focuses canonically on the argument and leaves the Bishop's illogical supposition in the dust:

> I deny any knowledge that "an excommunicated Lefebvre bishop Richard Williamson," "performed *contra iure* (sic) illicit confirmation" "on May 1987". While I am aware that Monsignor Lefebvre and the four bishops he consecrated in June, 1988, seem to have been declared excommunicated and schismatic, I am not aware that anyone else associated with them has also been so deemed to be declared excommunicated and schismatic, nor am I aware that the Holy See has expressly declared the "Pius X movement" formally schismatic. I am aware that under the reformed 1983 *CODE OF CANON LAW* an excommunicate is no longer *vitandus*.[256]

To encapsulate, first ,Bishop Ferrario argues Morley and company are schismatic because the Church declared the Pius X movement *schismatic*. A Vatican judgment of this sort has never been discovered.

Second, Bishop Ferrario asserts that having a radio program that disagrees with him is schismatic, all the more banal under the "freedoms" of Vatican II. To find this so is also

---

255 Letter from Patricia Morely, to Joseph A. Ferrario, *Bishop of Honolulu* (January 18, 1991).
256 Letter from Patricia Morley, to Joseph A. Ferrario, *Bishop of Honolulu* (January 18, 1991).

false, since contrary opinion on matters not of faith and morals is not schismatic.

Third, that the confirmation conducted by Bishop Williamson, one of the four excommunicated, was evidence of complicity, since Williamson was named a schismatic, is patently false. Morley and company were neither accomplices or complicitors, even assuming the legitimacy of the excommunication in the first place.

Upon appeal to the Congregation for the Doctrine of Faith, Joseph Cardinal Ratzinger through Cardinal Caciavillian held the Decree of May 1, 1991 invalid:

> From the examination of the case, conducted on the basis of the Law of the Church, it did not result that the facts referred to in the above-mentioned Decree are formal schismatic acts in the strict sense, as they do not constitute the offense of schism; and therefore the Congregation holds that the Decree of May 1, 1991 lacks foundation and hence validity.[257]

While the Congregation held out the interdict penalty, it seems unlikely Bishop Ferrario will put himself in the embarrassing position twice. The St. Joseph Foundation, who aided in the canonical defense of the Hawaii Six, sums up the affair:

> Regardless of whether or not Ferrario is guilty of the various morals charges against him in the courts, the wanton destruction of Our Lady of Peace Cathedral, the liquidation of diocesan real estate assets, and so forth, he did commit an egregious abuse of eccle-

---

257 Letter from A. Caciavillian, *Apostolic Pro-Nuncio,* to Patricia Morley, (June 28, 1993).

siastical power by excommunicating six of his faithful without following canonical procedures.[258]

Canonists, representing the Hawaii Six portray this
sorry employment of Church discipline. To some, the injus-
tices have been numerous:

> Without a scintilla of evidence, Bishop Ferrario
> proclaimed six people guilty of schism, denied them
> due process, including the right of defense, and he
> ignored advice he sought from other canonists to
> pursue his critics.
> Several of the excommunicated have suffered the
> contempt of their families, loss of business, loss of
> standing in the community, and none of this should
> have ever happened.
> If the bishop felt offenses had occurred, he was
> free to involve a legitimate canonical penal process.
> But he was not free to judge them guilty of schism
> and excommunicate them with a stroke of the pen.[259]

As a result of this finding, some conclusions are possible:

> - Schism is *not* attachment to the traditional sac-
> raments and Mass.
> - Schism cannot be inferred from attendance at
> service of the Society of Saint Pius X.
> - Schism is not grounded on non-faith and morals
> disagreement.

---

258 Paul Likoudis, *Bishop Lifts Excommunications Imposed on Six Hawaii Catholics*,
      The Wanderer, July 29, 1993, at A-8.
259 Paul Likoudis, *Bishop Lifts Excommunications Imposed on Six Hawaii Catholics*,
      The Wanderer, July 29, 1993, at A-8.

Cardinal Joseph Ratzinger showed courage in the overturn of a ludicrous decree by strict legal adherence. Despite
the reversal of Bishop Ferrario, Pittsburgh's Bishop Donald
Wuerl has made a similar decree, only a week after the above
described overturn, proclaiming those attending a Society
chapel, *Our Lady of Fatima,* are schismatic.[260]

Hawaii and Pittsburgh are identical cases whose Bishops
exhibit a defective understanding of schism.

V. Conclusion

No matter what historical cases are reviewed, whether it
be the Olde Dutch Catholics, the Russian Orthodox, the
National Church of China, the Sedevacanists of Saint Pius V,
the Polish National Catholic Church, or the New Age Woman
Church, they all exhibit a rejection of not just ideas but also
of those empowered to lead and authorize. In unison, the
Papacy, the Primacy of Rome and the faith and moral teachings that emanate therefrom are rejected. In McGlynn, individual conscience substitutes for the Magisterial Sovereignty
of the Church. In Ferrario, schism means disagreement,
despite submission. In Taddei, a parallel church is joined. In
Ngo-dingh-Thuc, Rome has no Pope. In these cases, the
schismatic mind flourishes.

To equate these conducts with Marcel Lefebvre is faulty
reasoning. To formalize disobedience, right or wrong, into
a demonstrable conclusion or first principle about schism is
to reject the very notion of what a schism is. Cardinal Rosalio
Laro, President of the Pontifical of Commission of the
Authentic Interpretation of Canon Law, recognizes this distinction.

---

260 Note, *South Side Chapel Schism,* CXLIX Pittsburgh Catholic 1, 1-2 (Aug. 27,
     1993).

"The act of consecrating a bishop (without a papal mandate) is not in itself a schismatic act. In fact, the Code that deals with offenses is divided into two sections. One deals with offenses against religion and the unity of the Church, and these are apostasy, schism, and heresy. Consecrating a bishop without a pontifical mandate is, on the contrary, an offense against the exercise of a specific ministry," not a rejection of Papal Authority! And hence definitely not schism[261]

In this fashion, one can sensibly distinguish a two-part foundation in the determination of schism. One first disobeys. Second, one then denies the authority of party he disobeys. Fr. David Bellant is on target when he acclaims:

The first element, disobedience, then, constitutes the matter of schism, while its formality lies in the second part, i.e., denying the authority of the Pope. Hence, although schism necessarily involves disobedience, it can never be said that a mere act of disobedience is an act of schism.

Yet, over and over again, the Archbishop is said to have committed a schismatic act." This is absolutely false, as Cardinal Lara asserts, given the position within the Code of the penalty for consecrating a bishop without papal mandate.[262]

---

261 Note, *Persecution! The Attacks Against Catholic Tradition Continue: Excerpted from _The Wanderer_ and _Homiletic & Pastoral Review_*, XVI The Angelus 20, 23 (May 1993).
262 Note, *Persecution! The Attacks Against Catholic Tradition Continue": Excerpted from _The Wanderer_ and _Homiletic & Pastoral Review_*, XVI The Angelus 20, 23 (May 1993).

The question of canonical disobedience is a study to itself. Canonist Reverend Joseph Sheehan's brilliant study, *Canonical Obedience* is worthy of examination. Sheehan typifies obedience as action lacking an absolutist flavor:

> The obedience which a secular cleric must show his Bishop is not without limit, nor is it a blind or absolute obedience whereby the cleric is reduced to the status of a "yes-man" or an ecclesiastical puppet. In fact, Canon 425 explicitly states that those who are appointed to serve in the capacity of Diocesan Consultors must take an oath to perform their duties, best interests of the diocese, without respect for persons. There may arise circumstances where a priest may be duty bound to warn or remonstrate with the Bishop. It is no act of insubordination if a subject warns, or even remonstrates with his superior, who by forgetfulness of his office is endangering the important interests of the Church.[263]

The requirement of obedience is related to its object. In the *ratio* of Lefebvre, extraordinary measure was the only path to choose. Sheehan further recounts:

> In canonical obedience there is not demanded a conformity of the speculative judgment on the part of the cleric to the mind of the Bishop. Canonical obedience does, however, demand the conformity of the practical judgment to the order given. The command materially considered in itself may, at times, be imprudent or inopportune; but obedience to it does

---

263 Joseph G. Sheehan, The Obligation of Respect and Obedience of Clerics Toward Their Ordinary, 116-117 (1954).

not imply an approval of it as such on the part of one's speculative judgment.[264]

Disobedience permissibly arises out of necessity. This is how Marcel Lefebvre focused on the world around him. The corruption of the world made it impossible for him to easily obey any law that contributed to the downfall of the institutional Church. His attestation on the May 5, 1988 protocol must have been disengeous since it highlights the positive renewal (in an Orwellian sense) of Vatican II.

The wisdom of St. Thomas Aquinas shines through in this dilemma:

> *On the contrary,* it is written (Acts v. 29): *We ought to obey God rather than men.* Now sometimes the things commanded by a superior are against God. Therefore superiors are not to be obeyed in all things.
> *Therefore if the emperor commands one thing and God another, you must disregard the former and obey God.* Secondly, a subject is not bound to obey his superior, if the latter command him to do something wherein he is not subject to him.[265]

LEGAL HOLDING 5.1: That under the Code of 1917 the acts of consecration were not self-evident proof of the Archbishop's refusal to accept the authority of Rome and the Supreme Pontiff. Under Canon 1325.

---

264 Joseph G. Sheehan, The Obligation of Respect and Obedience of Clerics Toward Their Ordinary, 118 (1954).
265 St. Thomas Aquinas, 2 Summa of Theologica, "Question 104, Article 5", page 1645 (1947).

LEGAL HOLDING 5.2: That an act of disobedience cannot be equated to schism under either the 1917 or 1983 Code.

LEGAL HOLDING 5.3: That under the Code of 1983, Canon 751 and 1364, the act of consecration should not be construed as an act of schism.

LEGAL HOLDING 5.4: That under the Code of 1983, the penalty for schism, being *latae sententiae* excommunication is invalid and has no effect under Canons 751 and 1364.

CHAPTER 10

Schism by Extension and Implication

LEGAL ISSUE #6: Whether those who follow, give "allegiance" to, or attend traditional Mass and Sacraments offered by any member of the Society of Saint Pius X are by extension and implication automatically excommunicated and properly declared schismatic?

I. Schism and the Followers

If the Vatican reaction to the consecrations ever reached embarrassing heights, it did so in the declarations on the faithful left behind him. An estimated range, from 500,000 to 4,000,000, being followers of Lefebvre's mission, were, by implication, declared schismatic. More that 250 priests, nearly a thousand churches, schools and convents were juridically affected. "By the Decree of the Congregation and the Pope *Motu Proprio, Ecclesia Dei* deduction was posited:

Sacerdotes et Christifideles monentur ne schismaticae Domini Lefebvre actioni assentiantur, ne in eandem poenam incurrant.[266]	The priests and faithful are warned not to seek to adhere to the schism of Monsignor Lefebvre, because they would incur *ipso facto* the extremely grave penalty of excommunication.[267]

266 Lo Scisma Lefebvre, LXI Apollinaris: Commenarius Instituti Utiusque Iuris 529, 551 (Tarcisius Berone, ed., 1988).
267 Bernardin Gantin, *Decree of Declaration of Excomminucation of the Congregation of Bishops*, Inside the Vatican 12 (Aug./Sept. 1993).

England's Cardinal Hume, on June 30, 1988, declared that the consecration "gets the Archbishop and his *followers* in schism from the Catholic Church."[268]

Is this a legitimate and honest judgment? Let us grant the Archbishop was disobedient. Does his singular act impugn all who follow? Oratorian canonist T.C.G. Glover expresses astonishment at the Vatican's proclamation on followers:

> The phrases "followers of Archbishop Lefebvre," "Lefebvrist Mass centers," "Lefebvre priests" are frequently used. They imply that Archbishop Lefebvre is the head of the Society of Saint Pius X. He is not. Fr. Franz Schmidberger has been Superior General for five years and has district superiors under him. Even if the six bishops had been excommunicated for illegal consecrations and schism, it would not in itself affect the others. If a retired Benedictine bishop were to be excommunicated, it would not mean that Benedictines throughout the world, and those who hear Mass in Benedictine churches, were excommunicated. Excommunication is a penalty for those who commit certain crimes with full moral guilt, not a contagious disease![269]

The radicalness of this vicarious transfer is plainly manifest in the canonical action of the Hawaiian Bishop Joseph Ferrario and the most recent pronouncement of Bishop Donald Wuerl of Pittsburgh.[270] Bishop Ferrario's decree of May 5, 1991, finds personal schism in the Hawaii Six by trivialized association:

268 Note, *Archbishop Lefebvre, The Time for Decision*, 75 Canon Law Society, Great Britain & Ireland Newsletter 14, 38 (1988).
269 Antonio de Castro Mayer, *Declaration* in Is Tradition Excommunicated? Where is Catholicism Today?, 95, 100 (Society of Saint Pius X, ed., 1993).
270 Note, *South Side Chapel Schism*, CXLIX Pittsburgh Catholic 1, 1-2 (1993).

Crudely put, you knew him — you must be just like him. And, of course, you think exactly alike, and would do exactly the same things. Jumbled reasoning like this is indefensible. Why not indict *all* the members of a parish when their pastor is discovered to be, a pedophile. Why not? You knew him — you followed — you showed allegiance? The comparison is not intended to stun — but to edify, though this comparison is foundationally faulty since pedophilia is a grave and intrinsically evil act, while at its worst, the Archbishop's conduct is but a procedural error.

Catholic writer, Roger McCaffrey sees the global impact of Ratzinger's decision on the work of the Society:

Still, the implications of the Vatican's ruling are monumental.

Prima facie, it is not unreasonable to assume that a chapel using any priests of the SSPX, and a bishop who in 1988 was declared schismatic and excommunicated by the Pope, is a chapel to be avoided as schismatic. But if Rome still holds the SSPX to be in a state of schism, the Ratzinger ruling is an unusual way to show it.

On the other hand, if Rome by ruling "in favor" of the Honolulu Six is sending a signal to the SSPX that it is no longer considered schismatic, then the point in negotiations with the Lefebvre priests.

Implicitly, Rome's ruling *seems* to say that the scores of independent Tridentine "chapels" across the U.S. — I'd guess 150 or even 200 — which operate outside the knowledge of (or in defiance of) the local bishop, are also not schismatic. Even when they have

priests from the SSPX saying their Masses. *A fortiori,*
such chapels are not schismatic when they merely
have a priest who is an itinerant, a man who might
be an ex-member of the Jesuits or a diocese or
whatever.[271]

To impute the schismatic act and intent, assuming its
validity, requires that the followers adopt the principles of
schism. Thus, if in fact the Archbishop said, "I'm going to
consecrate because I don't believe in the Pope or the authority
of Rome", his intention would be schismatic. Even so, the act
could not be imputed to his followers unless that follower
declared a complimentary view. Canonist Geringer on *Bay-
erischer Rundfund,* on June 30, 1988, posed that dilemma in
the following overview:[272]

Frage: Muß ein Anhänger Le-
febvres, wenn er weiterhin der
römisch-katholischen Kirche angehören will, explizit erklären, nein, ich
hänge nicht mehr Lefebvre an?

Prof. G.: Nein, vorläufig glaube
ich nicht, weil es ja vorläufig keine
Lefebvre-Kirche gibt, d.h. die Leute
die ihm anhangen sind noch immer
katholisch. Wenn es eines Tages dazu
kommen sollte, daß Lefebvre eine von
Rom unabhängige Kirche gründen
sollte, und diese ihm angehören
wollten, dann wäre das eine andere
Sache.[273]

Question: Must a follower of
Lefebvre, if he later wishes to adhere
to the Roman Catholic Church, declare explicitiy, "No, I no longer follow Lefebvre"?

Prof. G.: No, not for the time
being, I think. As for the time being
there is no Lefebvre Church, i.e., his
followers are still Catholic. If one
day it would come to that, that Lefebvre would found a Church loose
from Rome, and these people would
follow him, that would be a totally
different matter.[274]

---

271 Roger McCaffrey, *What Does the Vatican Now Consider "Schismatic"?,* 2 Latin
    Mass 4, 4-5 (Sept.-Oct. 1993).
272 Das Musikjournal, Gespräch mit Prof. Geringer: Lefebvre (Sendezeit:
    Donnerstag, 30 Juni 1988).
273 Das Musikjournal, Gespräch mit Prof. Geringer: Lefebvre (Sendezeit:
    Donnerstag, 30 Juni 1988).
274 Das Musikjournal, Gespräch mit Prof. Geringer: Lefebvre (Sendezeit:
    Donnerstag, 30 Juni 1988).

In the absence of a mental or theological agreement, schism cannot be vicariously transfused as if it were a blood exchange.

Aside from the generic policy, some attention should be paid to both the procedural and substantive issues involved here.

II. Substantive Arguments Relative to the Schism of Lefebvre and Effect on Followers

To have any chance of holding the followers accountable, the substantive allegation against the Archbishop will have to be upheld. By now, it is lucidly apparent, that in a majority of the canonical issues posed, the Archbishop is solidly acquitted. Only as to the Code of 1917, now applicable, does the Archbishop bear responsibility and any imputability is limited to conduct in contempt of ecclesiastical authority or *publicum animarum damnum*. If schism is found in the actor — leader, and the followers ascribe to that act, they, too, are schismatic. No amount of twisted and contorted canon analysis can make this so in the case of Marcel Lefebvre and those who follow him. The reasons are myriad.

First, the act of consecration, by and in itself, cannot support a finding of grave imputability under the Code of 1983. While it is true that the act of consecration could not be excused by a limited theory under the 1917 Code, its provisions have been superseded by a far more lenient code. Count Neri Capponi sees through the looseness of the new when compared to the old:[275]

---

275 Note, *Church Law, Jargon-Free and Interview with Count Neri Capponi*, 2 Latin Mass Magazine 14, 15 (1993).

Well, from the point of view of its guidelines, the ideas on which it is founded — it's a good code, a very much better Code than 1917, which was too rigid and formal.

Of course, it has suffered from certain fads, which have come out of the one-sided interpretation of the decisions or the documents of Vatican II. And, therefore, in certain cases, the penal side is not satisfactory — it's much too lenient. But especially with progressive bishops, when it's a question of penalizing anybody who's a follower of tradition, they forget the Code of 1983 and they go by the Code of 1917. And sometimes they even invoke penalties which had been abolished by 1983, and which existed in 1917.[276]

This being true, our analysis has made clear that the acts cannot be imputable if extenuating circumstances exist — from grave fear to necessity. At both Canons 1323 and 1324, the Code expresses its liberality. The Code says what it says and those entrusted to discipline Lefebvre don't like it. Count Neri Capponi portrays their decision-making consternation:

But it's extremely difficult to contradict the obvious meaning of the code. You'd have to change the law, I should say. If the Pope said, "No, that's not what I meant," then he'd have to say what he meant.[277]

---

276 Note, *Church Law, Jargon-Free and Interview with Count Neri Capponi*, 2 Latin Mass Magazine 14, 15 (1993).
277 Note, *Church Law, Jargon-Free and Interview with Count Neri Capponi*, 2 Latin Mass Magazine 14, 15 (1993).

The Code of 1983 and its *novus habitus mentis* would resist the harsh extension to followers. Ladislas Orsy, so dearly attached to the 1983 Code, is a proponent of the dejuridizing movement:

> But those who have acquired this new attitude rooted in an inquiring mind can never again be mere lawyers. No matter if they are legislators, interpreters, or judges, if their business is to make, or improve, or explain laws, they will always be ready to move to a higher viewpoint, should the case so warrant it. That vantage point may be provided by theology, or philosophy, or history, or by any combination of the different branches of learning. From there, they will be able to see the legal norms in a broader context, raise new questions, discover new answers, and then integrate the same norms into the life of the community in a happy combination of old and new so that each and all can experience, taste, and enjoy the freedom that was given to us, citizens of the Kingdom.[278]

Within this atmosphere of accommodation, is it likely that a repressive penalty could be advanced? The humanizing, deinstitutionalizing trend in Church Canon law would hesitate to act with such juridical passion.   Canonist McDonough reflects:

> Penal law should be viewed with binomial fidelity and newness as part of a transitional stage of change that from a new vantage point engenders new questions and new answers. The *novus habitus mentis* for sanctions can be highlighted against this back

278 Ladislas Orsy, Theology and Canon Law: New Horizons for Legislation and Interpretation 17 (1992).

drop by investigating: (1) the requirements for applying sanc*tions as a last resort; (2) the altered praesumptio iuris* regarding liability for sanctions; and (3) fundamentals of the preliminary procedure for either administrative or judicial imposition or declaration of a sanction.[279]

The Archbishop's malice (dolus) in the act of consecration needs to be amply manifest. A deliberate intention to violate the law, by and through a free will, absent of extenuating circumstances is needed. This commentary proves sufficiently that under the 1983 Code, grave fear or necessity serves to either excuse imputability in whole or mitigate the penalties dispensed. While there is a presumption of imputability, its evidentiary weight is undermined by *"nisi aliud appareat"*. It is reasonably concluded that the Archbishop, by his beliefs, could rebut the presumption of imputability. Thus, under the Code of 1983, the Archbishop's imputability was excused. If this be so, a finding of schism in his followers is a *reductio ad absurdum*.

To summarize, the Archbishop's imputability is excused by:

1. grave fear
2. necessity
3. a lack of grave imputability

Therefore, a lack of substantive charges negates a charge of schism in the followers.

---

279 Elizabeth McDonough, *A Novus Habitus Mentis for Sanctions in the Church,* 48 The Jurist 727, 728 (1988).

III. Procedural Arguments as to the Schism's Effect on Followers

One other avenue to impute schism in the followers is potentially available — an argument as to complicity. Complicity is cooperation, conspiratorial favor, a tainted relationship with the wrongdoer. If we allow the *latae* penalties to stick, at least hypothetically, the complicity argument may extend penalties to third parties. 1983 Code Canon 1329 addresses the conspiratorial or accomplice question:

Canon 1329 - §1. Qui communi delinquendi consilio in delictum concurrunt, neque in lege vel praecepto expresse nominantur, si poenae *ferendae sententiae* in auctorem principalem constitutae sint, iisdem poenis subiciuntur vel aliis eiusdem vel minoris gravitatis.	Canon 1329 - §1. If the penalties established against the principal author are inflicted ones (ferendae sententiae), then those who collaborate to commit an offense through a common conspiracy but who are not expressly named in a law or precept are subject to the same penalties or to other penalties of the same or lesser severity.
§2. In poenam latae sententiae delicto adnexam incurrunt complices, qui in lege vel praecepto non nominantur, si sine eorum opera delictum patratum non esset, et poena sit talis naturae, ut ipsos afficere possit; secus poenis *ferendae sententiae* puniri possunt.[280]	§2. Accomplices who are not named in a law or in a precept incur an automatic penalty (*latae sententiae*) attached to an offense if it would not have been committed without their efforts and the penalty is of such a nature that it can punish them; otherwise, they can be punished by inflicted penalties (*ferendae sententiae*).[281]

Of interest here is §2 (*latae sententiae*) which states that penalties are imposed automatically to accomplices. For the sake of debate, did the act of consecration take place because of followers? Look closely at §2.

It Would Not Have Been Committed Without Their Efforts.

---

280 Code of Canon Law, Canon 1329 (1983).
281 Code of Canon Law, Canon 1329 (1983).

Is this so? Were the followers inextricably tied to the act of consecration? Did they incite, solicit, elicit, coerce the Archbishop to perform the act? Did they plan, as if in a conspiratorial setting, the deed in question? To so hold is a farfetched deduction.

For the moment, let's consider 1329 §2 as to the four bishops consecrated. Would the act have been possible except for them? Would consecrations have occurred except for episcopal needs? If the act is evaluated without any reference to extenuating circumstances, is it fair to conclude that the four Bishops were imputed followers? Cardinal Gantin stated:

> I declare that in accordance with these laws the above mentioned Archbishop Marcel Lefebvre, Bernard Fellay, Bernard Tissier de Mallerais, Richard Williamson and Alfonso de Galarreta have *ipso facto* incurred excommunication *latae sententiae* reserved to the Holy See.[282]

The Pontiff mentions their names as *ipso facto* accomplices.

By the preponderance of evidence, a majority of canonical precepts, and an overwhelming majority of canonical authorities, Archbishop Marcel Lefebvre *and* his followers were not properly excommunicated *latae sententiae* for an act of consecration, or in classifying the act of consecration as *schismatic.*

---

282 Note, *Archbishop Lefebvre, The Time for Decision,* 75 Canon Law Society, Great Britain & Ireland Newsletter 14, 38 (1988).

As to the ordained bishops, assuming the validity of the original penalties imposed, an accomplice theory has limited merit. However, our studies look at the canonical improprieties in the issuance of these penalties, which make any vicarious judgment inane.

A similar type of analysis would occur under the 1917 Code.[283]

Therefore, it is improper to hold the followers of Marcel Lefebvre schismatic.

LEGAL FINDING 6.1: That, under the spirit of the 1983 Code, sanctions are to be used as a last resort, and in the case of Marcel Lefebvre, *latae sententiae* excommunication for schism was used too readily against him and even more so against of his followers.

LEGAL HOLDING 6.2: Due to excuse, extenuating circumstances or other mitigating cause, no schism or schismatic act and its attached *latae sententiae* excommunication would be imputable to the Archbishop and thus by extension to his followers.

LEGAL HOLDING 6.3: That the followers of Marcel Lefebvre are neither accomplices nor conspirators in the act of consecration, and as a result have no penalty imposed even assuming the Archbishop's penalties were legitimate.

283 Code of Canon Law, Canon 2205 (1917).

CHAPTER 11

Summary of Legal Issues and Legal Findings

By extraordinary evidence, the excommunication of Archbishop Marcel Lefebvre and a declaration of schism lacks canonical regularity. To some, including this author, anger and frustration had much to do with in dispensing the penalties against the Archbishop. St. Thomas Aquinas recognizes this probability as a motivation when declaring:

> First, on the part of its author as when anyone excommunicates through rage or anger, and then, nevertheless, the excommunication takes effect, though its author sins.[284]

For the Archbishop and his followers, this excommunication was not only canonically erroneous, it was unjust -- lacking in cause. St. Thomas describes a null excommunication scenario that fits perfectly in the case of the Archbishop:

> Secondly, on the part of excommunication, though there being no proper cause, or through the sentence being passed without the forms of law being

---

284 St. Thomas Aquinas, 3 Summa Theologica, Benzinger Brothers, New York Question 21, Article 4, page 2643 , (1947).

observed.[285]

In a case of substantive weakness or procedural irregularity argues St. Thomas, the declaration is made invalid and the excommunication declared a nullity. The conclusions listed below undoubtedly exonerate the late Archbishop Marcel Lefebvre.

LEGAL ISSUE #1: Whether imputability can be discerned or determined solely from the action of Archbishop Marcel Lefebvre?

LEGAL HOLDING 1.1: That imputability cannot be discerned or determined by a sole or singular examination of the action of Archbishop Marcel Lefebvre. Imputability has both subjective and objective elements under the 1917 and 1983 Codes.

LEGAL HOLDING 1.2: That the act of consecration requires a simple dolus, an errant belief that justifies the wrong, making proof of intent an easier burden under both the 1917 and 1983 Codes.

LEGAL HOLDING 1.3: That under the Code of 1917, it might be argued successfully that the Archbishop was imputable under a *Culpa* theory, that is, acted negligently in carrying out the consecration.

LEGAL HOLDING 1.4: That under the 1983 Code the external violation alone will not suffice, even under simple dolus, if the Archbishop can explain conditions that *nisi aliud appareat*.

---

285 St. Thomas Aquinas, 3 Summa Theologica, Benzinger Brothers, New York Question 21, Article 4, page 2643, (1947).

LEGAL ISSUE #2: Could a finding of initial imputability on the part of Archbishop Marcel Lefebvre, be excused, exempted or excepted by extenuating circumstances or conditions?

LEGAL HOLDING 2.1: Therefore, given the express restriction of contempt of ecclesiastical authority cases under Canon 2229 §3, and Canon 2205 as a means of excuse, exemption or mitigation of the act of consecration makes the Archbishop imputable under the 1917 Code of Canon Law.

LEGAL HOLDING 2.2: Any contempt of ecclesiastical authority denies the defense of grave fear or necessity making the Archbishop imputable under the 1917 Code, at Canon 2229 §3.

LEGAL HOLDING 2.3: Grave fear and necessity could remove imputability if the action of the Archbishop did not *"animarum damnum vergat"* under the 1983 Code, at Canon 1323, 4°.

LEGAL HOLDING 2.4: That the Archbishop's demonstration of fear, either grave or slight, could mitigate and diminish his imputability according to Canon 1324, 4° (1983).

LEGAL HOLDING 2.5: That the Archbishop's demonstration that his belief, as to fear and necessity of action, was held in good faith, even if erroneously, is a basis for diminished imputability under Canon 1323, 4° and 5°.

LEGAL HOLDING 2.6: That the Archbishop's proof of mitigating factors, such as fear, grave hardship, necessity, as an impetus to the consecration, will result in diminished imputability as provided in

Canon 1324 at 2°, 4°, 5°, 8°, 10°, and 12°.

LEGAL HOLDING 2.7: That the Archbishop's demonstration of any of Canon 1324's factors diminishing responsibility, will mitigate a *latae sententiae* penalty under Canon 1324 at 2°, 4°, 5°, 8°, and 10°.

LEGAL ISSUE #3: Whether the Archbishop's act of consecration, without papal mandate, can be excused on account of fear, or in the alternative, be a means to diminish imputability.

LEGAL HOLDING 3.1: That under the Code of 1917, fear, whether grave or slight, will neither remove nor diminish imputability for the act of consecration by the Archbishop Marcel Lefebvre was listed as an damaging to the salvation of souls at Canon 2205 and 2229.

LEGAL HOLDING 3.2: That under the Code of 1983 grave fear, and even relative fear, as manifested by his action and word, will remove imputability for his actions, if they do no harm to souls as enunciated at Canon 1323, 4°.

LEGAL HOLDING 3.3: That under the Code of 1983, at Canon 1324, 5°, 8° and 10°, the *latae sententiae* excommunication if declared valid, would be diminished or mitigated by the existence of fear.

LEGAL ISSUE #4: Whether necessity can excuse or mitigate the Archbishop's imputability for the unauthorized act of consecration.

LEGAL HOLDING 4.1: That under the Code of 1917, the Archbishop's action of consecration would not be justified by necessity since his action was in contempt of Church authorities and listed as an offense causing damage to souls under Canons 2205 and 2229.

LEGAL HOLDING 4.2: That under the Code of 1983, the act of consecration would be justified by necessity given the state of the Church and remove all imputability since his action did not "verge on harm to souls" under Canon at 1323, 4°.

LEGAL HOLDING 4.3: That under the Code of 1983, the act of consecration would not result in full imputability since the agent believed he was justified by the current state of the Church under Canon 1324 4°, 5° and 10°.

LEGAL ISSUE #5: Whether the Archbishop's act of consecration, without papal mandate, is an act of formal schism.

LEGAL HOLDING 5.1: That under the Code of 1917 the acts of consecration were not self-evident proof of the Archbishop's refusal to accept the authority of Rome and the Supreme Pontiff. Under Canon 1325.

LEGAL HOLDING 5.2: That an act of disobedience cannot be equated to schism under either the 1917 or 1983 Code.

LEGAL HOLDING 5.3: That under the Code of 1983, Canon 751 and 1364, the act of consecration should not be construed as an act of schism.

LEGAL HOLDING 5.4: That under the Code 1983, the penalty for schism, being *latae sententiae* excommunication is invalid and has no effect under Canons 751 and 1364.

LEGAL ISSUE #6: Whether those who follow, give "allegiance" to, or attend traditional Mass and Sacraments offered by any member of the Society of Saint Pius X are by extension and implication automatically excommunicated and properly declared schismatic?

LEGAL FINDING 6.1: That, under the spirit of the 1983 Code, sanctions are to be used as a last resort, and in the case of Marcel Lefebvre, *latae sententiae* excommunication for schism was used too readily against him and even more so against of his followers.

LEGAL HOLDING 6.2: Due to excuse, extenuating circumstances or other mitigating cause, no schism or schismatic act and its attached latae sententiae excommunication would be imputable to the Archbishop and thus, by extension, to his followers.

LEGAL HOLDING 6.3: That the followers of Marcel Lefebvre are neither accomplices nor conspirators in the act of consecration, and as a result have no penalty imposed even assuming the Archbishop's penalties were legitimate.

PROTOCOL OF AGREEMENT BETWEEN
THE HOLY SEE AND THE PRIESTLY
SOCIETY OF SAINT PIUS X

Signed in Rome on May 5, 1988.

I. Text of the Doctrinal Declaration

I, Marcel Lefebvre, Archbishop-Bishop emeritus of Tulle, as well as the members of the Priestly Fraternity of Saint Pius X founded by me:

1. Promise to be always faithful to the Catholic Church and the Roman Pontiff, her Supreme Pastor, Vicar of Christ, Successor of Blessed Peter in his primacy as Head of the Body of Bishops.

2. We declare our acceptance of the doctrine contained in number 25 of the Dogmatic Constitution *Lumen Gentium* of the Second Vatican Council on the ecclesial Magisterium and the adherence which is due to that magisterium.

3. With regard to certain points taught by the Second Vatican Council or concerning later reforms of the liturgy and law, and which seem to us able to be reconciled with the Tradition only with difficulty, we commit ourselves to have a positive attitude of study and of communication with the Holy See, avoiding all polemics.

4. We declare in addition to recognize the validity of the Sacrifice of the Mass and the Sacraments celebrated with the intention of doing that which the Church does and according to the rites indicated in the typical editions of the Roman Missal and the Rituals of the Sacraments promulgated by Popes Paul VI and John Paul II.

5. Finally, we promise to respect the common discipline of the Church and ecclesiastical laws, especially those contained in the Code of Canon Law promulgated by Pope John Paul II, without prejudice to the special discipline granted to the Society by particular law.

II. Juridical Questions

Keeping in mind the fact that the Priestly Society of Saint Pius X has been conceived for 18 years as a society of common life — and after studying the propositions formulated by His Excellency Marcel Lefebvre and of the conclusions of the Apostolic Visitation carried out by His Eminence Cardinal Gagon — the most suitable canonical form is that of a Society of apostolic life.

1. Society of Apostolic Life

This is a solution which is possible under canon law, and it has the advantage of allowing the insertion of laypeople into the clerical Society of apostolic life (for example, cooperating Brothers).

According to the Code of Canon Law promulgated in 1983, canons 731-746, this Society enjoys full autonomy, can form its members, can incardinate clerics, and can assure the common life of its members.

In the proper Statutes, with flexibility and inventive possibility with respect to the known models of these Societies of apostolic life, a certain exemption is foreseen with regard to the diocesan bishops (cfr. can. 591) in matters having to do with public worship, the *cura animarum* [care of souls] and other apostolic activities, keeping in mind canons 679-683.

As for jurisdiction with regard to the faithful who have recourse to the priests of the Society, it will be conferred on these priests either by the local Ordinaries or by the Apostolic See.

2. The Roman Commission

A commission to coordinate relations with the different Dicasteries and diocesan bishops, as well as to resolve eventual problems and disputes, will be constituted through the care of the Holy See, and will be empowered with the necessary faculties to deal with the questions indicated above (for example, implantation of a place of worship, at the request of the faithful, where there is no house of the Society, *ad mentem* can. 683. par. 2).

This commission will be composed of a President, a Vice-President and five members, of whom two will be from the Society.

Among other things it would have the function of exercising vigilance and lending assistance to consolidate the work of reconciliation and to regulate questions relative to the religious communities having a juridical or moral bond with the Society.

3. Condition of Persons Connected to the Society

3.1. The members of the clerical Society of apostolic life (priests and cooperating lay brothers) are governed by the Statutes of the Society of Pontifical Right.

3.2. The oblates, both male and female, whether they have taken private vows or not, and the members of the Third Order connected to the Society, all belong to an Association of the faithful connected with the Society according to the terms of Canon 303, and collaborate with it.

3.3. The sisters (that is, the Congregation founded by Mons. Lefebvre) who make public vows: they constitute a true institute of consecrated life, with its own structure and autonomy, even if a certain type of bond is envisaged for the unity of its spirituality with the Superior of the Society. This Congregation — at least at the beginning — would be dependent on the Roman commission, instead of the Congregation for Religious.

3.4. The members of the community living according to the rule of various religious Institutes (Carmelites, Benedictines, Dominicans, etc.) and who are morally bound to the Society: these are to be given, case by case, a particular statute which will regulate their relations with their respective Orders.

3.5. The priests who, as individuals, are morally connected to the Society, will receive a personal statute taking into account their aspirations and, at the same time, the obligations deriving from their incardination. The other particular cases of the same nature will be examined and resolved by the Roman commission.

As for the laypeople who request the pastoral assistance of the communities of the Society: they will remain under the jurisdiction of the diocesan bishop, but — notably by reason of the liturgical rites of the communities of the Society — they will be able to turn to them for the administration of the sacraments (for the Sacraments of Baptism, Confirmation and Marriage, the usual notifications must still be given to their proper parish priest; cfr. can. 878, 896, 1122).

Note: The particular complexity of two questions must be kept in mind:

1. The question of the reception by laypeople of the sacrament of Baptism, Confirmation and Marriage in the communities of the Society;

2. The question of the communities which practice the rule of this or that religious Institute without belonging to it.

It will be in the competence of the Roman commission to resolve these problems.

4. Ordinations

For ordinations, two phases must be distinguished:

4.1. *Immediately:*

For the ordinations scheduled to take place in the immediate future, Archbishop Lefebvre would be authorized to confer them or, if he were unable, another bishop accepted by him will be authorized.

4.2. *After the erection of the Society of apostolic life:*

4.2.1. In so far as possible, and within the judgment of the Superior General, the normal path is to be to be followed: to send dimissorial letters to a bishop who agrees to ordain members of the Society.

4.2.2. In light of the particular situation of the Society (cfr. *infra*): the ordination of a member of the Society as a bishop, who, among other responsibilities, would also be able to proceed with ordinations.

5. The Problem of the Bishop

5.1. On the doctrinal (ecclesiological) level, the guarantee of stability and maintenance of the life and activity of the Society is assured by its erection as a Society of apostolic life of pontifical right, and the approval of its Statutes by the Holy Father.

5.2. But, for practical and psychological reasons, the consecration of a member of the Society as a bishop seems useful. This is why, in the context of the doctrinal and canonical solution of reconciliation, we suggest to the Holy Father that he name a bishop chosen from among the members of the Society, presented by Archbishop Lefebvre. In consequence of the principle indicated above (5.1), this bishop as a rule is not the Superior General of the Society. But it seems opportune that he be a member of the Roman commission.

6. Particular Problems (to be resolved by decree or declaration).

— Lifting of the *suspensio a divinis* on Archbishop Lefebvre and dispensation from the irregularities incurred by the fact of the ordinations.

— *Sanatio in radice*, at least *ad cautelam*, of the marriages already celebrated by the priests of the Society without the required delegation.

— Prevision for an "amnesty" and an accord for the houses and places of worship erected — or used — by the Society until now without the authorization of the bishops.

Joseph Cardinal Ratzinger
Marcel Lefebvre

EXCOMMUNICATIONS

(The asterisk designates excommunications of greater importance, which are considered in Section 2, below.)

Canon	Brief Designation of Crime	How Reserved
2341, § 1	*Apostasy, heresy, schism	a) *In foro conscientiae,* specially to Holy See b) *In foro externo,* to the Ordinary
2318, §1	*Special books (publishing, defending, reading, keeping)	specially to Holy See
2318, § 2	*Scripture printed without permission (author; publisher)	*nemini*
2319, §§ 1-4	*Marriage before minister; (also non-Catholic education or baptism)	to the Ordinary
Conc. Balt. n. 124	*Marriage after civil divorce	to the Ordinary
2320	*Profanation of sacred Species	most specially to Holy See
2322, 1°	Mass or confession without priestly orders	specially to Holy See
2326	Relics (falsification, sale, unlawful public exposition)	to the Ordinary

*Asterisk designates the most practical cases.

2327	Traffic in indulgences	simply to Holy See
2330	Crimes in papal election	most specially to Holy See (Document I[1))
2332	Appeal from Pope to Council	specially to Holy See
2333	Recourse to lay authority to impede papal documents	specially to Holy See
2334, 1°	Laws contrary to liberty or rights of Church	specially to Holy See
2334, 2°	Recourse to lay authority to impede ecclesiastical jurisdiction	specially to Holy See
2335	*Masonic societies	simply to Holy See
2338, §1	Presuming to absolve from excommunications l. s. specially or most specially reserved	simply to Holy See
2338, §2	Communication with vitandus	simply to Holy See
2339	Ordering or compelling ecclesiastical burial of excommunicated or interdicted person	nemini
2341	*Summoning higher Prelate before lay tribunal	specially to Holy See

---

1 Superceded by Const. Ap., Vacantis Apostolicae Sedis, 8 Dec., 1945; AAS

2341	*Summoning Prelate lower than own Bishop before lay tribunal	simply to Holy See
2342	*Various violation of papal cloister	simply to Holy See
2343, §1	*Laying violent hands on Roman Pontiff	most specially to Holy See
2343, §§2, 3	*Laying violent hands on Cardinal and others down to titular Bishop	specially to Holy See
2343, §4	*Laying violent hands on cleric or religious	to culprit's own Ordinary
2345	Usurping property or rights of Roman Church	specially to Holy See
2346	Confiscation of church property	simply to Holy See
2347	Alienation without *beneplacitum*	*nemini*
2350	*Abortion	to the Ordinary
2351, §1	Dueling	simply to Holy See
2352	Compulsion to clerical or religious state	*nemini*
2360, §1	Forgery of papal documents	specially to Holy See
2363	*False accusation of solicitation	specially to Holy See

2367, §§1, 2	*Absolving *complex in peccato turpi*	most specially to Holy See
2368, §2	*Failure to denounce for solicitation	*nemini*
2369, §1	*Direct violation of seal	most specially to Holy See
2385	*Apostasy from religion	a) clerical exempt, to his own major superior b) lay or non-exempt, to Ordinary of place
2388, §1	*Marriage with sacred orders or solemn vows (accomplices also)	simply to Holy See
2388, §1 (Dig. 2, pp. 579, 580)	*Same in case of priest who who cannot separate	most specially to Holy See
2388, §2	*Marriage with simple perpetual vows	to Ordinary
2392	Simony in office, benefice, etc.	simply to Holy See
2405	Tampering with episcopal documents	simply to Holy See
AAS, 42-553	Teaching children what is contrary to faith and morals	specially to Holy See
AAS, 42-330	Violating canon 142 *(negotiatio)*	specially to Holy See

| AAS, 42-601 | Plotting against ecclesiastical authorities, occupying office, etc. | specially to Holy See |
| AAS, 43-217 | Consecrating a Bishop not appointed nor expressly confirmed by the Holy See | most specially to Holy See |

SUSPENSIONS

Canon	Brief Designation of Crime	Nature and Reservation[2]
671, 1°	*Religious of perpetual vows dismissed for minor crimes	general, reserved to Holy See
2341	*Summoning cleric or religious before lay tribunal	from office, reserved to Ordinary
2366	Presuming to hear confessions without jurisdiction	*a divinis*, not reserved
2366	Presuming to absolve from reserved sins	from hearing confessions, not reserved
2370	Consecrating Bishop without mandate	general, reserved to Holy See
2371	Simony in reception or administration of sacraments	general, reserved to Holy See

2 These suspensions are censures unless marked as vindictive penalties.

2372	Receiving orders from one under censure	*a divinis*, reserved to Holy See
2373	Various illegal ordinations	from conferring orders (vindictive, 1 year), reserved to Holy See
2374	Illegal reception of orders	from order so received, not reserved
2386	*Religious fugitive in sacred orders	general, reserved to own major superior
2387	Religious in sacred orders, fraudulent profession	general (vindictive) reserved to Holy See
2394, 3°	Chapter admitting official unlawfully in possession	from right to elect, etc. (vindictive), reserved to Holy See
2400	Resigning office to lay person	*a divinis*, not reserved
2402	Abbot or Prelate *nullius* failing to receive blessing	from jurisdiction, not reserved
2409	Vicar Capitular illegally granting dimissorial letters	*a divinis*, not reserved
2410	Violating right of Ordinary in ordination of religious	from celebration of Mass (vindictive, 1 month), not reserved

INTERDICTS

Canon	Brief Designation of Crime	Nature and Reservation
2332	College appealing from Pope to Council	specially to Holy See
2338, §3	Permitting divine services in interdicted place	from entry into church, not reserved
2338, §4	Giving cause for local or collective interdict	personal, not reserved
2339	Giving ecclesiastical burial to excommunicated or interdicted person	from entry into church, reserved to Ordinary

About the Author

Charles P. Nemeth, Esquire, has extensive experience in both the practical and scholarly applications of the law. Educated at George Washington University, Duquesne University, the University of Baltimore, Niagara University, and the University of Delaware, Mr. Nemeth is a member of the Pennsylvania and North Carolina Bar Associations, the Association of Trial Lawyers of America, the Academy of Criminal Justice Sciences and the National Association of College and University Attorneys. He is currently Director and Professor of Public Service Administration at Waynesburg College in Waynesburg, Pennsylvania.

He is currently a Ph.D. candidate at Duquesne University concentrating on Catholic moral philosophy and the natural law of St. Thomas Aquinas. Mr. Nemeth is a widely published author whose texts number more than 20, by Prentice Hall, John Wiley and Sons and Anderson Publishing Company, and has also written articles in scholarly journals including his recent work entitled, <u>A Commentary on the Natural Law, Moral Knowledge and Moral Application</u>.

As an attorney, Mr. Nemeth has been active in all aspects of civil and criminal litigation for more than sixteen years. At present, his office specializes in matters involving education law, tax interpretation, personal injury, and corporate mergers and acquisitions.

Mr. Nemeth, a practicing Catholic, resides in Rosslyn Farms, Pennsylvania with his wife of 23 years, Jean Marie, and seven children: Eleanor, Stephen, Ann Marie, Joseph, John, Mary Claire, and Michael.